Contents

SELECTED POEMS

AFTER THE FALL

PITT POETRY SERIES

Ed Ochester, Editor

AFTER THE FALL

poems

old

and

new

EDWARD FIELD

University of Pittsburgh Press

Published by the University of Pittsburgh Press, Pittsburgh, Pa., 15260

Copyright © 2007, Edward Field

All rights reserved

Manufactured in the United States of America

Printed on acid-free paper

10 9 8 7 6 5 4 3 2 1

ISBN 13: 978-0-8229-5980-9

ISBN 10: 0-8229-5980-1

for Diana Athill

from *A Frieze for a Temple of Love,*
Poems 1993–1997 (1998)

NEW
POEMS

What Poetry Is For

Credo

What good is poetry
if it doesn't stand up
against the lies of government,
if it doesn't rescue us
from the liars that mislead us?
What good is it
if it doesn't speak out, denounce what's going on?
It's nothing
but harmless wordplay to titillate and distract—
the government knows it
and can always get rid of us if we step out of line.

That I believed in poetry,
even when I betrayed it,
that I came back to its central meaning
—to save the world—
this and only this
has been my own salvation.

after C. Milosz

Homeland Security

My advice to anybody who looks like an Arab these days is,
when you're in a post office or jogging around the reservoir,
never stop and jot down any notes,
even if it's a great idea for a poem.
And for God's sake don't snap any photos at the airport,
even of your cousins arriving from St. Louis.
God forbid you should draw a map of the subway for them,
showing the route between their hotel and your house!

And if a new "friend"—the guy on the next bar stool, say—
starts suggesting pranks
like blowing up tunnels or poisoning the water supply
or, God forbid, assassinating anyone
and how it might be done by you and a few pals,
just keep saying what's fun about that,
even as a reality game, and you're really only
interested in poetry about nightingales.

And if this "friend" brings up the subject of the Palestinians,
for whom you might reasonably have some sympathy,
and asks how about joining up to help in resisting the occupation,
or aren't you furious about the takeover of Iraq,
and don't you want revenge, he can get some weapons—
just choke back your rage and go vague,
become a dumb American and say Iraq? Where's that?

Don't be surprised if photographs and taped conversations—
did you think that button on your "friend's" shirt
was just a button?—are used against you
as evidence that you're a terrorist mastermind
plotting to overthrow the government
and install an Islamic Republic here—

even if he's the one who laid out the plot
and all you did was cross your eyes.

So even if you'd love to get rid of the criminals
in the government of this, your adopted country,
as bad as the ones you escaped from
who jailed your father for years without trial,
just cultivate a stupid grin and play dumb.

And when they lead you away in handcuffs
don't bother protesting your innocence and calling for a lawyer.
You can't have one—and you're guilty.

Letter on the Brink of War

for Diane and Olivia

Dears,

You're already painting the porch? You ladies are up early.
And you say the frogs are croaking away in the pond?
How normal it all sounds.

Here too it's spring, and after the worst winter in years,
the weather is heavenly,
which makes the crisis all the more ghoulish.

I can't wait to get out of here.

In the face of monstrous events,
everything I have to do, shaving, shopping, for instance,
seems so trivial.

But looking back from the future at our time,
I already know how delicious, how foolishly ordinary,
such trivialities will seem.
In retrospect it will seem amazing
—if we survive—
that we could go about our normal lives,
even zombie-like,
with this hanging over our heads.
But it only hits me now and then.
Mostly, I want to go to bed and stay there,
as if that could make this go away—
you never get enough sleep in wartime.

It's one of those points in history
that everything turns on—
I keep thinking I should put everything down,

right now, record it while it's hot,
but I don't feel up to it.

It's so much like the thirties, it's scary—
the Bush election, like Hitler getting in with a minority vote,
and a gang of psychopaths taking over the government, etc.,
then turning the country into a war machine,
with the military at the service of corporate interests.
And 9/11 our Reichstag fire,
and them using it to scare us to death.

They even talk of shock and awe—
another term for blitzkrieg's sturm und drang—

and instead of Jews, the roundup of Muslims.
But you have to ask, Who's next?

Catastrophic, maybe, for those they label Evil,
but our lives, too, will never be the same—
payback time is coming.

A Brazilian friend says
it's like the takeover of the Colonels in her country,
with armed soldiers patrolling streets,
railroad stations, bus terminals, subways, etc.

It's not just that our government is doing openly
what it has always done covertly—
regime change in the interests of the rich
has always been our specialty.

But now that they have the excuse for it—
the war against terrorism, as they once cowed the country
with the threat of subversives in our midst—

and it's the end of democracy at home,

the constitution shelved.
Civil rights? Don't make me laugh.
When we protest, it's going to become a war against us.
They have an insane goal—to rule the world—
and the military might to get there.
Iraqi oil will pay for it all? Ha-ha.

Is it a hopeless dream that, someday, a court,
like the one at Nuremberg that tried the Nazis,
will bring these criminal psychopaths to justice?
They must not escape. This is our vow.
But it might be too late to restore the world they destroyed.

Right now, how I want to hear those frogs in your pond,
so sane, so normal—still.
Will they be croaking
if we come next year?

And dare we talk about the future?

Love, Eddie

Good-bye to Berlin

From my air base in England during the war
it took us half a day to Berlin in our lumbering bomber
and another half day back.
Now, a half century later, making the same trip
this time as a tourist on a budget airline,
it's an hour and a half each way,

and instead of spreading havoc as before,
I walk off the plane with my bag
and take the train to a hotel in the center
we once kept our Norden bombsights aimed at,
but actually dropped our loads anywhere—
carpet bombing, we called it.

On my first air raid on Berlin
I ended up in the chilly waters of the North Sea—
it was February. This time it's June,
and I'm not shot down, merely overwhelmed
with the blackbirds singing their little hearts out,
the jasmine-like scent of the linden trees in flower,
and air that's unpolluted like no other capital city—
the famous Berliner *luft*.

Whatever the rights and wrongs of the bombing—
and a good case can be made either way—
it was the bombs that stripped the buildings
of their ponderous baroque trimmings and, when restored,
made them so light and handsome.

You're still ready to bolt for the borders
—no way to forget the Nazi nightmare—
but for now the population's pussycats, as civilized as anyone,

the men's deep voices almost purring
the harsh syllables of a language
that once terrified the world with its nightmare
of cruelty and death.

It was that that justified, not only for our strategists
but for me, bombing this city to rubble,
and at the time nobody cared
that it was full of women and children and their pets,
as now we have conquered and occupied Iraq
on the grounds that, like the Nazis, it threatened
the rest of the world with destruction.

Again I hear the boast of pinpoint bombing
with a minimum of civilian casualties—regrettable mistakes—
but whatever they say, our brave, simple-minded warriors,
the country is in ruins
just as it would be if we carpet-bombed it. . . .

This was not Nazi Germany
but the only Muslim country in the Middle East
with a secular government, the best run of them all.
Maybe that's not saying much,
but it's finished, probably forever,
with the fever of religious fundamentalism let out of the bag.
I'd go crazy too, with this greedy gang taking over,
whose only interest is their own—
a bunch of oilmen and construction tycoons
out to make fortunes.

Amazingly, it was Germany that stood up
against this piratical invasion.
Perhaps it is the Germans' turn to teach Iraq
the art of democracy that we have lost—
but we'd never give them the chance.
With the same organization they rebuilt their country out of ruins,

they'd be brilliant at directing the reconstruction of Iraq
and straightening out the mess we've made of it.
Though on second thought, remembering past efficiencies,
maybe too efficient—but it does take a ruthless streak
to get things done.

I always longed for Baghdad,
a great city where life was good once,
though it's Berlin I'd rather live in
and German I'd rather speak.
How good the language feels in my mouth,
even my out-of-date phrase-book sentences—
the book dates from after the war. Alas,
I'll never get the chance to ask anyone
if they have taken part in an *angriffe*,
a word that makes an air strike like the clawing of a tiger.
I've also learned to say *Ich war flieger*,
though I feel it's more discreet not to,
or worse, to ask someone if he was an *U-boot kommandant.*

I can enjoy the wonderful life they again live,
with full consciousness of the past—
in fact that's what makes it so thrilling to be here—
the drama of the past is everywhere.
Would I stay in Berlin if I could? It's academic, at my age—
maybe another visit, but essentially this is good-bye.
And it's ironic that it has taken me all these years,
over so many visits, to fall in love with Berlin so fatally.
Good-bye, good-bye, wonderful city.
Starting with an act of hate, we struggled through the years,
until at last, in the end,
Berlin, you won.

My Favorite President

"What would you do if a Nazi was raping your sister?"
"Interpose myself between them, of course."

He was like all of us
who grew up on
D. H. Lawrence and Henry Miller.

Still waving the banner of Sexual Freedom,
he demonstrated that nothing stops you,
you don't let anyone or anything,

not even with the CIA out to catch you at it,
interrupt your sex life—
whatever the price.

He is the only president
I wouldn't mind
going down on.

Listen, a friendly, good-looking guy like him?
Sure, I'd suck that man's dick—
anybody would.

Can you imagine doing it with any of the others—
Nixon? Harry Truman?
George Washington? Honest Abe?

He's the first one in two hundred years
who looks like
he'd really enjoy it,

just a healthy southern boy
who loves to lie back
and be done thataway.

And most of the country
feels just like me—
that he's got a right,

and even if he lies his head off when caught in the act,
swears on a stack of bibles,
we still want him to get away with it.

In Memory of My Foreskin

Alone, when I whang off,
I like to imagine you're still there,
as if you're necessary, even ghostlike,
for full enjoyment.
But I couldn't remember you, not possibly,
since they separated us
in the maternity ward.

Somehow I still miss you
or feel that something is missing.
Not that I've been shortchanged,
though I haven't been over-endowed either.
It's just that without your protection
I'm generally retracted, perhaps in memory of the knife—
anyone would shrink at the thought of it—
and I regret the advantage, slight as that is,
you'd have given me in the school showers,
proudly displaying myself in all my glory
before the uncut boys.

Being in a state of contraction,
I can't help but feel a twinge of envy
at the beauty of a full-swinging dong.
Within the shelter of the foreskin
the helmet cap is freer to radiate
its glamorous energy.
Some are prettier than others,
sheathe membranes thin and silky,
and some are longer than necessary—
I knew a man who had one fit for a horse,
giving the illusion of length
without the substance.

It *is* a loss, undoubtedly, though a minor one,
but, ah, the task of life
is to deal with What Is,
not with What Should Have Been,
and as a Jew I can't say I regret the sacrifice,
part of the ancient contract we, as infants,
make with our parents, our tribe, our history—
leading to years of therapy, of course.
That's also part of the package,
which either destroys you,
or if you're lucky, you survive
to learn essential things about
the limitations of belief,
and the mystery.

Let's say about the bargain
that the advantages in the long run
outweigh the disadvantages.
It's the price to pay for being a Jew,
and, ultimately, in spite of all the kvetching,
I'm more of a man for it.

Holding Up the Universe

The most thrilling thing in the world
is grabbing a guy's dick.

After all, it's the realest, the most
alive, intense, and sensitive part of a man.

No bullshit.
You get right to him.

He might see it as a threat
and kill you, of course,

or, on the other hand, let it happen,
and open up to you.

Once, a Zen master ordered his acolyte
to take his position, holding up the universe,

from which nothing was supposed to budge him, nothing—
when the master grabbed his balls.

The acolyte told me the story
later in California.

They're all gay, he said,
and left the monastery forever.

But when he demonstrated his position for me,
holding up the universe,

I was tempted to reach for his balls myself,
so I couldn't tell him what I really thought,

that the master had demonstrated the work ahead for him,
to shed his last defense—

unnecessary in that context, at least—
protecting his balls.

Oedipus Schmoedipus

It is the bitter truth
that everyone marries their mother.
Or, rather, after some years
your mate turns into your mother.
And the incest prohibition kills the lust
that brought you together in the first place.

But if you have become my mother, sweetheart,
and I've become yours,
we're both at least taking care of each other
with a son's devotion.
An odd coupling of two quite strange mothers,
joining hands in holy matrimonio?
This is a recipe for incompatibility, I'd say.

As your Jewish mother
I find you a difficult child
who will not listen, when all I'm doing
is trying to get down into you
some chicken soup to keep you alive.
Then in a rage at your defiance,
I'm transformed into your father
and want to kill,
as the oedipal prescription demands:

Lying there stabbed to death,
my tender victim, my dearest one,
crying Mama, Mama,
and the maternal heart responds,
breaks for him, my child, *mein kind*, again,
and, unaccountably, my mother,
whom I knock myself out to rescue
from the inevitable, familial mistake.

If This Be Jews

Now that Jews are no different from anyone else,
do we have to prove it by being as bad as anyone else?
Of course, why shouldn't Jews be as bad as anyone else?
Who says we have to be better?
Except of course, we're Jews. . . .

You used to have to be at least a genius
in order to beat the quotas at Ivy League colleges—
I'm afraid I wasn't, and couldn't,
when I tried to get into Columbia.
We weren't even considered Caucasian—we were Semites,
and in my town that meant practically Negro.

But that was before Israel.
My God, how life changed for us. .
The Restricted signs came down from hotels,
and they practically begged us to join the country club.
Now we can live in the classiest neighborhood,
and like real Americans
play tennis, go skiing in Aspen.

There were always token Jews in every field,
but after Israel, Jackie Kennedy
even invited New York Jewish Intellectuals to the White House
and made us celebrities—I say *us* because they were us, the tribe.
What any Jew does is on all our merit badge sashes.

That may have been the first step on the downward path,
for at the same time, other Jews were being persecuted as reds,
and those inner-circle Jews were silent about it or approved.
To our credit, outsider Jews like Allen Ginsberg
shot their mouths off. He had a big mouth.

George W. even includes Jews in his war cabinet—
probably so we could be blamed if anything went wrong,
as it has—tragically, though predictably, wrong.
But what are Jews doing in this government?
Wasn't civil liberties always a Jewish passion?
Could Jews really be for invading other countries,
locking people up in cages without a trial,
sending them to other countries to be tortured?
How can any Jew send the army out to conquer the world
for McDonald's and Halliburton and Standard Oil,
not to speak of occupying for forty years
a people no worse, no better than us
and grinding them into the humiliating dust?

Nobody ever said it was going to be easy being a Jew,
but if these be Jews, I want out,
except, sorry, Jewboy, you can't defect—
Hitler taught every one of us that.

Too Late

Too late to hire a boat and break into attics
where the trapped are standing with water up to their necks

too late to set up the grid plan over the city
and assign a rescue crew to each square

too late to set up the emergency phone network
that would have helped everybody know what was going on where

too late to get everybody out of the city before the hurricane struck
as Fidel Castro did

way too late to have a coherent plan
to organize the whole rescue operation

don't even talk about it's too late
to put money into the dikes, the wetlands,

instead of pouring billions into failed savings and loans, the
pharmaceutical industry,
the oil war in Iraq, the forty-year occupation of the Palestinians

but it's not too late to stand Bush and his gang
up against the wall.

Mission Accomplished

Bill Clinton just had it naturally,
but George W.'s got a surefire enhancer,
the parachute harness pulling up between his legs.

It's like wearing a tool belt, or the dangling telephone—
once you're seen in this getup,
you're a real gun-toting American.

Your real gun-toting American loves him—
sure, they can see it's an act,
but it's the same as theirs.

Like the cowboy accent and swagger kids put on, not to be sissies,
and grow out of, or else end up no-goodniks, in jail,
not usually the presidency.

It's an appropriate costume
for a dyslexic, cocaine-snorting frat boy
whose daddy bought him oil wells and a baseball team,

who never had to win an honest election,
whose crowing Mission Accomplished
announced the beginning of America's humiliation,
the hurricane that his agenda has brought on us.

Don't be fooled by the parachute harness.
The truth is that bunched up between the straps
there's nothing there.

What Poetry Is For

in homage to Ernesto Cardenal

Back in the seventies, when a Nicaraguan poet
came to the Poetry Center in New York and read his poems
about the United Fruit Company with the help of the U.S. government
robbing his people and terrorizing with death squads,
most of the audience of poetry lovers walked out.
I was there, I saw it—
they just didn't want to listen.

Or were brainwashed.
They were probably scared because he was a communist
and they'd be accused of being subversives,
so it was safer not to listen
to what we were doing in Latin America—
practice for what we're doing a hundred times over
in half the world today.

But his poetry, spoken out of the anguish in his heart,
was trying to make us hear—
even if the truth is ugly.
And dangerous.

It was also beautiful
that he told us, flat out, in the simple language of truth,
what we were doing to his country.

Now, too, what else for a poet to write about
except the devastation and misery
our so-called democratic country is causing,
not only at home, with a government turning the economy
into a grab bag for the wealthy,

but abroad, where we've become the Evil Empire,
sending pirate armies to the ends of the earth
to take over governments, seize their assets and control markets,
leaving anarchy behind us,
creating hatred wherever we go and dangerous enemies
who can fly planes with breathtaking accuracy
into our arrogant towers,
who devote themselves to wrecking our lives
as we've wrecked theirs.

One poet I know is saying it plainly like the Nicaraguan did.
Richard Vargas in Albuquerque writes about the war in Iraq,
"we're going to be paying for this for a long time
probably way past my lifetime.
we've screwed generations to come,"
(here he's talking about the soaring national debt)
"and i wouldn't be surprised
if they let us starve in the streets in our old age."

That's how poets should be writing in this critical time.
And about the pathology of our leaders
who call everyone who opposes them a terrorist,
even if the cause is just—people fighting against
the occupiers of their lands, against our armies of corporate greed.

And if any of us says, No! No more of this!,
we're reminded of their awesome power—
"if you're not with us you're against us."
We know what that means—
there's a Guantanamo Bay in our future.

Vargas, my poet friend, says the most important thing right now:
"if we elect [that chickenshit] bush again the world community
will shun us for the fucking idiots we are."

But how to get rid of this gang
if the voting machines are rigged?

And why aren't more poets shouting from the rooftops?
Or at least from the stages of all the Poetry Centers?

As a British diplomat said, "If this continues,
all we can look forward to is unending war."

The stark reality. The warning. What a poet's for.

Judgment at Nuremberg

It was only when the cars were marooned in garages,
everyone shivering because heating oil was unavailable,
and crowds of the starving broke into food warehouses and markets,

when inflation had wiped out savings and made pensions meaningless—
jobs? forget it!—
and with the country sunk into the deepest depression in its history

that everyone finally woke up as if from a dream
and saw the criminal clique they had put their trust in,
that had destroyed their lives.

Even the Christians who believed they had someone
in the White House on their side finally knew
it was just rich men, oilmen in particular,
who had used their pentecostal ideas, cynically,
to fill their own pockets.

The government tried to rescue itself from the debacle
by declaring a holy war, not only on Terrorism,
but on the Muslim world.
This was suicidal, like Hitler from the bunker.

But the country was no longer listening.

The military initially tried to take over
by declaring a national emergency, but the soldiers weren't being paid—
they stayed only because they were being fed.

Even national television for once refused
to cooperate with Pentagon directives. People
just wanted their country back. No way, with the crippling national debt—

even with inflation it was overwhelming.
We owed the whole world for their money
that had kept the fake prosperity going for so long.

But now, who to believe? There were many
who offered to lead us to recovery, but they were tarnished
with their support of the disgraced administration
and its disastrous wars in the Middle East.

The Christian Right had its zombie army,
and other militias sprang up around the country.
It looked like the South was finally going to break away from the rest,
as it was prevented doing in the Civil War.

That's when the country got behind the UN and the World Court,
setting up a tribunal to try our leaders.

Fantasy? They're going on trial, just you wait.

Dead Man Walking

Dead Man Walking

If you think it's a shock reaching thirty,
just wait till you turn eighty.
Eighty, I keep saying to myself,
I'm eighty and life's quite normal—
still walking around, still jacking off.

Of course, one spill and I could be
in the Village Nursing Home that I pass every day.
We're waiting for you, the attendants' faces say,
as they enjoy their cigarettes on the sidewalk
or chat on their cellphones.
And the wrecks in wheelchairs out front
look at me grimly as I lope by, which I read as,
You think you're so smart, Pops,
you'll soon be right here, with us.

Actually, it's been months since my birthday,
and I'm still taking it in,
and when the crucial event happens
I imagine it will also be awhile
before I wake up and realize where I am—
in a wheelchair, hospital bed, or coffin.

In Praise of My Prostate

While most men I know are having theirs irradiated,
scooped out, or surgically removed,
we're enjoying a blissful Indian Summer.

The more horror stories I hear
the more I'm determined to hold on to you—
you're my own and I want you just the way you are.

Yes, I pee all night like any guy my age,
and if I'm rarely rock hard anymore,
I'm not complaining—

rock hard's often numb as a stone,
whereas you're a living bulb,
if bulbously encrusted by our long voyage,

and you still expand, your amazing flowers
bursting forth throughout my body,
pistils and stamens dancing.

When It Struck Him

The man at a table in the café
cried, *Je suis vieux.*
This happened in Paris.
Again and again he cried out,
Je suis vieux, je suis vieux!
then laid his head down in his hands
and began to sob.

Everybody at their tables
or standing at the counter
looked around and stared.

The *patron* watched anxiously
from his post at the cash register
as the man continued to sob loudly.
A waiter rushed over
and put a hand on his shoulder,
handed him a brandy,
which he gulped down,
then automatically reached for money to pay.
No need for that, the waiter said in French,
and helped him to his feet
and out to the sidewalk.

The man stood there a minute
blinking in the flat light,
shrugged, blew his nose,
and walked to his fate.

Taking My Breath Away

Even at the age of seventy, he takes my breath away.
I fell in love with his mother at ninety,
so this family has staying power.

Yes, around other people he can look drawn and old,
but in private he sheds his clothes and his age
to become the charming boy I met at the office
where we were temporary typists and the supervisor
made the mistake of sitting us next to each other—
we talked so much she soon put us
at opposite ends of the typing pool.

Too late, we were hooked,
and I brought him to meet my analyst,
who came from generations of rabbis
and pronounced her blessings on us.
Her ancestors must have turned over in their graves!

Strange that someone who looks so healthy
can have such dread diseases—
brain tumors, seizures, and now the wobbles—
but they don't affect his essential beauty,
which keeps taking my breath away,
as when I first caught sight of his pop-up penis
making the enchanting bulge in his pants.

I wasn't wrong about it—it was special,
and he was too, though too volatile to hold down.
Unlike me, he was organized and scheduled,
which put my sloppiness into harness,

if ultimately to wait on him hand and foot.
I can't complain, that was my destiny.

Over forty years later he's still in my life,
and I'm still dazzled, the luckiest man alive,
the man with everything.

Mrs. Wallace Stevens

My poor Neil has to put up with me
like Wallace Stevens' wife, who finally had enough
of the famous-poet act and drew a line
through the center of the house—
on one side of it his domain, the other side hers,
making her a freak in the eyes of history, while Stevens
it celebrates as the ultimate aesthete,
poet of chamber music, the Master.

The trial of living with a poet—
I sympathize with her totally, as I'm sure Neil does too:
we're all ego and career-driven and every once in a while
deserve a good kick in the ass,
fat ass in the case of Wallace, skinny in mine.
Who better justified to let loose with a good one
than the long-suffering partner, especially Mrs. Stevens,
living with a grandee of the poetry world,
making his high and mighty pronouncements,
the poems playful and charming and musical, yes, but . . .
as if his socks didn't smell and no skid marks on his underwear—
she held her nose picking them up from where he dropped them.
That part of his life never got into his poetry,
in his infuriating way taking his comforts for granted—
life's bourgeois pleasures all there just for him.

Ah, I could have told her he was the typical poet,
no worse a snob, no more selfish
than the rest of us. Or maybe just a little more.
But with her dividing line through the house,
Mrs. Stevens formalized the great poet's split
between his dirty underwear and his mind, the line
that goes right through his poetry as well.

And if she simmered, she stood by her choice,
the lowlier, if more human, role, as my dear Neil does—
it's one of the things I admire him for, his sense of his own territory,
refusing to be intimidated by my self-important poetry scene,
though in our case, not drawing any line—
luckily, since we live in one room,
not the sprawling suburban home of our most genteel of poets.

If Mrs. Stevens terrorized Wallace in her own way,
I'm sure he adored her even more for it, as I do you, sweetheart,
for her resistance, her stubborn defiance,

for she did for him what nobody else could,
what he kept secret from the world—
no, not wash his socks and underwear, which was just her part of
        the bargain—
she made him laugh.

Prospero, in Retirement

Turbulent events over, the tropical island
a gruesome memory,
I am a private citizen again
with a sufficient if ungenerous pension
provided by our good Uncle,

and, while awaiting the sequence of surgeries
expected in my age group,
just like all the other oldies in the supermarket
pushing their shopping carts—
or maybe luckier,
since unlike many of them,
angry-faced and aggressive with their carts in the aisles,
I'm not alone.

I hardly can remember when,
all those years,
I had a public responsibility—
for what, to save the world?
Stimulate unawakened minds?
Straighten out erroneous ideas?
I no longer imagine I could!
But I had healing magic in my fingertips then,
and the voices of the gods encouraged me.
I even dreamed that Shakespeare created
me, the Magician.
And when the words that came from him
appeared on the page,
I *was* Shakespeare!

Only when I go on stage to do my old act,
—with the hall three-quarters empty,

as it usually is now—
do I remember how important this once was to me,
and I am jolted back into the heady atmosphere
of performance, of significance, of revelation,
where the words matter
and I'm able to connect
to the heart and soul of people again—
God, those poems are good!
And I forget I'm just another old guy
with a leaky prostate and a shopping cart.

Back in my private life,
I won't read anymore
about Kosovo, Chechnya, Africa.
After a lifetime of horrors
that basket is full and there's no room
for another massacred innocent.
I am more and more cut off from the world,
except in the warm embrace
of my home with my wonderful friend—
so lucky, so lucky, wouldn't you say?—
or on my travels abroad,
where I am still connected to something greater
than shopping and cooking and cutting hair—
The Seven Wonders of the World, truly,
The Great Adventure, The Quest, which goes on
but has to end soon
when these limbs grow too frail
to totter to the plane.
But as long as I can get
my ass and my wheelie to Kennedy Airport,
I'll keep going, keep going, keep going. . . . .

After the Fall

After the Fall

No one in his right mind could truthfully say that he liked a vast edifice. . . . At the most we gaze at it in wonder, a kind of wonder which in itself is a form of dawning horror, for somehow we know by instinct that outsize buildings cast the shadow of their own destruction before them.

—from *Austerlitz*, by W. G. Sebald

I too disliked them
—the way they wrecked the classic New York skyline—
and plotted how to get rid of them,
or at least cut them lower.

Merely an irritation before,
now after their fall
they've grown monstrous,
looming over our lives.

I despised them
but never thought that others,
with more reasons perhaps, not just aesthetics,
hated them even more.
And hate created a plan—so simple,
but mightier than the high-tech might
of the atom bombs, the missile shields
we threaten the world with,

and with a ruthlessness we're also capable of,
but also an intelligence,
a complexity, we lack.

✳

When the phones started working again,
sympathy calls came from all over,
even from Berlin
that we carpet bombed in the war.

I bombed it myself —five times—
plus Cologne, Hamburg,
and a couple dozen other cities.
And felt justified.

Now they're sorry for us.

※

Here, in the Frozen Zone, where I live,
cut off from the rest of the city by a police barrier,
it's almost like Cold War Berlin,
the constant sirens, our war planes roaring over,
though not breaking the sound barrier like then—
the Ossies said we did it on purpose to intimidate them.
In Berlin, if I was twisted in a yoga posture,
the crack of a plane breaking the sound barrier
made me jump
and nearly broke my back.

Now I listen, expecting the roar overhead
to be another attack.

※

A diabolical thought about the plan,
its total success—

once they thought of it, it was so beautiful
they had to do it.

Forget the reasons.
Sure, it grew out of hatred, rage, a need for vengeance, whatever,
but it became a work of art they were obsessed by—
it had to be achieved.

Once thought of, it was so beautiful
they had to do it.

Then, all their reasons fell away—
when you think of something so perfect,
you've got to do it.

Suddenly I have tears in my eyes.

But who would understand
in this terrible time?

✳

I never would have believed
they were so fragile.
I never could have imagined
the fragility of those buildings
that stood in their solid ugliness for years.

And who would ever have expected them
to go down like that, like a shot,
dissolve before our eyes,
when all our fantasies of disaster
pictured them leaning awry.

Our innocence is, finally, gone—
this has shattered it—
and now we are aware of the fragility
of everything we depend on:

our political institutions,
which were already shaken by evidence
of how elections are stolen

and our traditions of freedom, limited
under the guise of "protecting" us.

The fragility of our economy
        that depends on control of the world's oil,

and can collapse if we don't shore up governments
        good or bad
and destroy others, whether good or bad.

Fragility—facing life
without electricity
        no heat
        no hot water—those long, delicious showers
        no light
        no cooking stove
        no record player
and worst of all, no computer.

Maybe we never deserved to have so much in the first place.

                *

It isn't the first time towers have collapsed.
Remember the Tower of Babel?
The Colossus of Rhodes?
And the cathedral builders
whose attempts crashed down for centuries,
according to my art history prof in college,
until they discovered the flying buttress to shore them up.
The Leaning Tower of Pisa represented success, of a sort.
Perhaps we could look at the latest flop
in a historical context and say,
Better luck next time?

                *

I don't call these terrorists—
they're religious fanatics,
and we have plenty of those ourselves,
storing up guns, bombing abortion clinics,
and sending bombs and anthrax threats in the mail.

We bomb countries to smithereens
and aren't called terrorists.

Now it's "terrorists" we're after,
but the hunt will widen,
fed by what frightens the witch-hunters in their dreams,
to the old category of "subversives"—
those who don't salute the flag fast enough,
who think for themselves,
who object to punishing the innocent to disguise
our failure to catch the guilty.

It's opened a new era.
Our bunch
has a free rein,
and they're even more dangerous.

✳

*It really happened, I keep saying, and see
the jetliner gleaming white in the morning sun
hit the tower. . . .*

✳

How to digest it?
I'm a mile north of Ground Zero
with a direct view of the smoking gap,
the wound in the heart of the financial district skyline.
I can't stop looking south along the river,

and I keep walking down there, the grit under my feet.
It is awesome—
smoke billowing out of the rubble like the fumes of hell,
long, arcing sprays of water over it,
blackened hulks of buildings around, a graveyard.
Thousands are dead in that pile of rubble,
their pulverized bones in the grit under my shoe soles.

The whole financial district feels like a dying neighborhood.
It will be a long time
before anyone will want to work there again.

Airfields know better than to group their planes on the tarmac.
While the politicos are mouthing upbeat messages
about recovery of the financial district,
the corporations are quietly dispersing.
The fanatics knew what they were doing
when they shot down Nelson and David,
destroyed the twin temples
of the Rockefellers, who controlled the world's oil, the money,
and kept women in shrouds, children starving,
and turned men desperate enough to do these deeds.

*

Christians at least should understand them
martyring themselves for their religion,
for what they see as justice.
Didn't the Christians in ancient Rome
offer themselves to the lions?
And Christian martyrs through the ages
are celebrated as holy ones,

even if they didn't kill thousands with them
on their trip to paradise.
Though Christians have themselves tortured and slaughtered
millions of infidels without a qualm.

*

In Afghanistan, I climbed a bare outcropping
in the middle of green Bamian valley,
where leopards prowled the fields,
guarded by giant Buddhas carved into the valley's stone walls.
They were spared by the invading armies of Genghis Khan
but in our own era were dynamited by religious fanatics.

Eight hundred years ago, that hill I stood on
was a bustling town, a proud town in this rich valley,
until it was demolished

by Genghis Khan in his sweep across Asia.
All its inhabitants were killed
for resisting his army.

Nobody has ever excavated it,
even for the treasures within.
It's still a place of horror, a forbidden place.
Only goats graze there.

Eight hundred years ago, but they will never forget.
They leave it to the winds and grasses.
And lizards.

Also appropriate now.
Just leave it.

       ✳

I don't even want to think of
      those inside the planes
as they headed toward the towers

I don't want to see the planes
      crashing into them
the fuel exploding

I don't want to think any more of those
trapped on the high floors
waving from the windows

I don't want to see
      the people jumping
hand in hand

I don't want to think of
      the firemen running up the stairs to save them

not knowing, nobody knowing
      the buildings were going to fall
      first one tower collapsing in dust
then the other

I don't want any of this to happen
      but it plays over again and again
         in my mind

      ✳

When the Colossus of Rhodes fell
the ancient world shuddered—
the gods had spoken.

Then the gods
were dead.

They fell,
and mankind had to live with it,
with the fragments that were left,
with the heaps of rubble
we pray over.

SELECTED

POEMS

from *Stand Up, Friend,*

With Me (1963)

Hydra

This island whose name means water
Never had gods and temples as other Greek islands had;
It never was the home of monsters with ferocious heads,
And maybe it wasn't even there.

But a few centuries ago,
As though it had just risen from the sea,
Men saw stones and pine trees on the slopes
And with the stones made houses and with the trees made ships.

And as naturally as fish swim
The ships went sailing;
And as naturally as the sun rises
The boys grew into heroes and sailed to war.

But the heroes were foolhardy as heroes are,
So although they were brave and did amazing things
The ships were sunk at last
And the handsome heroes lay on the ocean floor.

Wars over, fame won, the island settled down,
But with the trees all gone the soil blew away to sea;
The houses began to crumble,
And the island bleached in the sun to anonymity.

The name means water, but now even the wells are drying
And no one expects the rock to grow trees again,
While the waters push gently on its shores
Waiting for the island to sink quietly back in the sea.

Donkeys

They are not silent like workhorses
Who are happy or indifferent about the plow and wagon;
Donkeys don't submit like that
For they are sensitive
And cry continually under their burdens;
Yes, they are animals of sensibility
Even if they aren't intelligent enough
To count money or discuss religion.

Laugh if you will when they hee-haw
But know that they are crying
When they make that noise that sounds like something
Between a squawking water pump and a foghorn.

And when I hear them sobbing
I suddenly notice their sweet eyes and ridiculous ears
And their naive bodies that look as though they never grew up
But stayed children, as in fact they are;
And being misunderstood as children are
They are forced to walk up mountains
With men and bundles on their backs.

Somehow I am glad that they do not submit without a protest,
But as their masters are of the deafest
The wails are never heard.

I am sure that donkeys know what life should be,
But, alas, they do not own their bodies;
And if they had their own way, I am sure
That they would sit in a field of flowers
Kissing each other and maybe
They would even invite us to join them.

For they never let us forget that they know
(As everyone knows who stays as sweet as children)
That there is a far better way to spend time;
You can be sure of that when they stop in their tracks
And honk and honk and honk.

And if I tried to explain to them
Why work is not only necessary but good,
I am afraid that they would never understand
And kick me with their back legs
As commentary on my wisdom.

So they remain unhappy and sob,
And their masters who are equally convinced of being right
Beat them and hear nothing.

Prologue

Look, friend, at this universe
With its spiral clusters of stars
Flying out all over space
Like bedsprings suddenly busting free;
And in this galaxy, the sun
Fissioning itself away,
Surrounded by planets, prominent in their dignity,
And bits and pieces running wild;
And this middling planet
With a lone moon circling round it.

Look, friend, through the fog of gases at this world
With its skin of earth and rock, water and ice,
With various creatures and rooted things;
And up from the bulging waistline
To this land of concrete towers,
Its roads swarming like a hive cut open,
Offshore to this island, long and fish-shaped,
Its mouth to a metropolis,
And in its belly, this village,
A gathering of families at a crossways,
And in this house, upstairs and through the wide open door
Of the front bedroom with a window on the world,
Look, friend, at me.

A Journey

When he got up that morning everything was different:
He enjoyed the bright spring day,
But he did not realize it exactly, he just enjoyed it.

And walking down the street to the railroad station
Past magnolia trees with dying flowers like old socks—
It was a long time since he had breathed so simply.

Tears filled his eyes and it felt good,
But he held them back
Because men didn't walk around crying in that town.

And waiting on the platform at the station
The fear came over him of something terrible about to happen:
The train was late and he recited the alphabet to keep hold.

And in its time it came screeching in,
And as it went on making its usual stops,
People coming and going, telephone poles passing,

He hid his head behind a newspaper,
No longer able to hold back the sobs, and willed his eyes
To follow the rational weavings of the seat fabric.

He didn't do anything violent as he had imagined.
He cried for a long time, but when he finally quieted down
A place in him that had been closed like a fist was open,

And at the end of the ride he stood up and got off that train:
And through the streets and in all the places he lived in later on
He walked, himself at last, a man among men,
With such radiance that everyone looked up and wondered.

A View of Jersey

Notes from a Slave Ship

It is necessary to wait until the boss's eyes are on you,
Then simply put your work aside,
Slip a fresh piece of paper into the typewriter,
And start to write a poem.

Let their eyes boggle at your impudence;
The time for a poem is the moment of assertion,
The moment when you say, I exist,
Nobody can buy my time absolutely.

Nobody can buy me even if I say, Yes, I sell.
There I am sailing down the river,
Quite happy about the view of the passing towns,
When I find that I have jumped overboard.

There is always a long swim to freedom.
The worst of it is the terrible exhaustion
Alone in the water in the darkness,
The shore a fading memory and the direction lost.

2
A Bill to My Father

I am typing up bills for a firm to be sent to their clients.
It occurs to me that firms are sending bills to my father
Who has that way an identity I do not often realize.
He is a person who buys, owes, and pays,

Not papa like he is to me.
His creditors reproach him for not paying on time
With a bill marked "Please Remit."
I reproach him for never having shown his love for me
But only his disapproval.
He has a debt to me too,
Although I have long since ceased asking him to come across;
He does not know how and so I do without it.
But in this impersonal world of business
He can be communicated with:
With absolute assurance of being paid
The boss writes "Send me my money"
And my father sends it.

3
The Telephone

My happiness depends on an electric appliance
And I do not mind giving it so much credit
With life in this city being what it is
Each person separated from friends
By a tangle of subways and buses
Yes my telephone is my joy
It tells me that I am in the world and wanted
It rings and I am alerted to love or gossip
I go comb my hair which begins to sparkle
Without it I was like a bear in a cave
Drowsing through a shadowy winter
It rings and spring has come
I stretch and amble out into the sunshine
Hungry again as I pick up the receiver
For the human voice and the good news of friends

4
The Statue of Liberty

All the ships are sailing away without me.
Day after day I hear their horns announcing
To the wage earners at their desks
That it is too late to get aboard.

They steam out of the harbor
With the statue of a French woman waving them good-bye
Who used to be excellent to welcome people with
But is better lately for departures.

The French gave her to us as a reminder
Of their slogan and our creed
Which hasn't done much good
Because we have turned a perfectly good wilderness
Into a place nice to visit but not to live in.

Forever a prisoner in the harbor
On her star-shaped island of gray stones
She has turned moldy looking and shapeless,
And her bronze drapery stands oddly into the wind.

From this prison-like island
I watch the ships sailing away without me
Disappearing one by one, day after day,
Into the unamerican distance,

And in my belly is one sentence:
Set Freedom Free,
As the years fasten me into place and attitude,
Hand upraised and face into the wind
That no longer brings tears to my eyes.

Sonny Hugg and the Porcupine

This baby porcupine squeezing into a crevice of rock
Could be hauled out into the open,
Poked with a stick, and otherwise toyed with,
But cute as he was he couldn't be kissed.

Love rose tender in the heart of Sonny Hugg,
And he dreamed impossible dreams.
But all those bristles! His mind twisted and turned
To find a workable solution.

To hug this improbable child was important to him,
The child willing or no, and who could say it wasn't willing.
Maybe the Gillette, the garden shears . . . No, without those spurs
This creature would be unlovable as a rat.

Sonny was versatile, but this defeated him.
He faced reality. A porcupine for a lover?
Alas, he would have to settle for those creations
Not quite as darling but with bodies good for hugging.

Graffiti

Blessings on all the kids who improve the signs in the subways:
They put a beard on the fashionable lady selling soap,
Fix up her flat chest with the boobies of a chorus girl,
And though her hips be wrapped like a mummy
They draw a hairy cunt where she should have one.

The bathing beauty who looks pleased
With the enormous prick in her mouth declares,
"Eat hair pie; it's better than cornflakes."
And the little boy in the Tarzan suit eating white bread
Now has a fine pair of balls to crow about.

And as often as you wash the walls and put up your posters,
When you go back to the caged booth to deal out change
The bright-eyed kids will come with grubby hands.
Even if you watch, you cannot watch them all the time,
And while you are dreaming, if you have dreams anymore,

A boy and girl are giggling behind an iron pillar;
And although the train pulls in and takes them on their way
Into a winter that will freeze them forever,
They leave behind a wall scrawled all over with flowers
That shoot great drops of gism through the sky.

Unwanted

The poster with my picture on it
Is hanging on the bulletin board in the post office.

I stand by it hoping to be recognized,
Posing first full face and then profile,

But everybody passes by and I have to admit
The photograph was taken some years ago.

I was unwanted then and I'm unwanted now.
Ah guess ah'll go up Echo mountain and crah.

I wish someone would find my fingerprints somewhere,
Maybe on a corpse, and say, You're it.

Description: Male, or reasonably so,
White, but not lily-white, and politically a pinko

Thirty-fivish, and looks it lately,
Five-feet-nine and one-hundred-thirty pounds: no physique

Black hair going gray, hairline receding fast,
What used to be curly now fuzzy,

Brown eyes starey under beetling brow,
Mole on chin, probably will become a wen.

It is perfectly obvious that he was not popular at school,
No good at baseball, and wet his bed.

His aliases tell his history: Dumbbell, Good-for-nothing,
Jewboy, Fieldinsky, Skinny, Fierce Face, Greaseball, Sissy.

Warning: This man is not dangerous, answers to any name,
Responds to love, don't call him or he will come.

The Sleeper

When I was the sissy of the block who nobody wanted on their team
Sonny Hugg persisted in believing that my small size was an asset
Not the liability and curse I felt it was
And he saw a use for my swift feet with which I ran away from fights.

He kept putting me into complicated football plays
Which would have been spectacular if they worked:
For instance, me getting clear in front and him shooting the ball over.
Or the sensation of the block, the Sleeper Play
In which I would lie down on the sidelines near the goal
As though resting and out of action, until the scrimmage began,
And I would step onto the field, receive the long throw
And to the astonishment of all the tough guys in the world
Step over the goal line for a touchdown.

That was the theory anyway. In practice
I had the fatal flaw of not being able to catch
And usually had my fingers bent back and the breath knocked out of me,
So the plays always failed, but Sonny kept on trying
Until he grew up out of my world into the glamorous
Varsity crowd, the popular kids of Lynbrook High.

But I will always have this to thank him for:
That when I look back on childhood
(That four psychiatrists haven't been able to help me bear the thought of)
There is not much to be glad for
Besides his foolish and delicious faith
That, with all my oddities, there was a place in the world for me,
If only he could find the special role.

At the Coney Island Aquarium:
   An Ode for Ookie, the Older Walrus Child
                     or
            The Sibling Rival

Do not worry, sweet little walrus, about the superior cuteness
Of those two new babies they brought to share your pool.

You keep pushing the twins out of the way
More concerned about keeping them from getting attention
Than having your own scrub-brush nose whiskers rubbed
So that no one gets the chance to give you
The endless hugs and kisses you deserve.

It is impossible of course to be more popular than twins
So finally you sink to the bottom and play dead
Hoping our hearts break—mine does anyway
And the Keeper watches anxiously, so you see it works.
But how long can you sit at the bottom of the water
When lungs cry for air and the heart for love?

No, Ookie, don't seek indiscriminate love from the many
As those two simple-minded children do
Who have not yet met with heartbreak (although they will),
But leap the railing right into my arms
And squirm there fishily always, Ookie, mine alone.

The Charmed Pool

At the charmed pool swarming with lower forms of life,
The flying, the crawling, the swimming, and the stationary,
Prince Charming looked around and wondered
Which of these creatures was the Princess
Who, the story said, was victim of a witch's curse
And waited for his kiss to reappear.

He was willing to try this kissing game
Even if a snake or a stone wasn't his idea of a good time.
To begin he chose a green frog with a gummy eye
And waded after it into the water feeling ridiculous
But with a sense of fulfilling prophecy.
Oh prince, prince, will you never grow up?

He caught the amphibian in his hand
And planted a kiss where he guessed its mouth was
And Prince Foolish, still pimpled from self-abuse,
Swooning with the same old admiration,
Was in his arms. He dropped him flat.
This magic can be an odd occupation.

He set about kissing all the creatures
Like the game of knock-knock-who's-there:
A dragonfly turned into Jack the Jew-Killer,
A mushroom into Miss Venom of the grammar school,
And soon there were lots of unpleasant people sitting around.
That witch had excellent taste in whom to banish.

Finally from a stone he got a princess,
Not his Princess to be sure, but the orphan princess,
With a calculated tear running down her nose
And crossed eyes that said, "Pity me."

He had, until he found her in the scullery with his uncle,
Praying at the head and sinning at the tail.

This had gone far enough; the Princess obviously wasn't there.
He took off his Prince costume
Revealing a quite attractive but ordinary young man
Who no longer knew what to do or where to go.
According to the story he found his princess at last
But, reader, do you really think he did?

This charming Prince who thought life had a happy ending,
I don't like to leave him like that naked by the pool,
The legend on the ground like a heap of wornout clothing.
But if I said anything definite it would just be made up.
When a man tries the charmed pool and fails
What can he do if he doesn't die of it?

Is he wandering about the forest waiting to be found?
By whom? For what? He'll be a heap of bones by then.
Did he find the road back to where he came from?
And learn like us to live from day to day
Eating what's to eat and making love with what's available?
And did he ever fall in love again?

Ode to Fidel Castro

I

O Boy God, Muse of Poets
Come sit on my shoulder while I write
Cuddle up and fill my poem with love
And even while I fly on billows of inspiration
Don't forget to tickle me now and then
For I am going to write on World Issues
Which demands laughter where we most believe.

Also, My Cute One, don't let me take a heroic pose
And act as though I know it all
Guard me from Poet's Head that dread disease
Where the words ring like gongs and meaning goes out the window
Remind me of the human size of truth
Whenever I spout a big, ripe absolute
(Oh why did you let the architects of our capital city
Design it for giants
So that a man just has to take a short walk and look about
For exhaustion to set in immediately)
Please, Sweet Seeker, don't discourage me from contradicting myself
But make everything sound like life, like people we like
And most of all give me strength not to lay aside this poem
Like so many others in the pile by my typewriter
But to write the whole thing from beginning to end
O Perfection, the way it wants to go.

II

My subject, Dear Muse, is Fidel Castro
Rebellissimo and darling of the Spanish-American lower classes

A general who adopted for his uniform
The work clothes of the buck private and the beard of the saints
A man fit for ruling a great nation
But who only has an island.

Irene, the beautiful Cuban, has his picture over her bed
Between Rudolph Valentino and the Blessed Virgin
He stands large and flabby between the perfect body and the purest soul
Doves on his shoulders, on his open hands
And one dove for crown standing on his head
He is not afraid of birdshit, his face is radiant.

Someday Hollywood will make a movie biography of his life
Starring the spreading Marlon Brando
They'll invent a great love on his way up, a blonde with a large crucifix
Whom he loses along with his idealism, and once at the top
A great passion, a dark whore with large breasts, to drag him down.
In real life his romance is with his people and his role
Otherwise his sex life is normal for his age and position.

Fidel, Fidel, Fidel . . .
I am in love with the spotlight myself
And would like the crowds to chant my name
Which has the same letters as yours but rearranged
Where is my island Where my people
What am I doing on this continent Where is my crown
Where did everyone go that used to call me king
And light up like votive candles when I smiled?
(I have given them all up for you sweet youth my muse
Be truly mine.)

Am I like Goethe who kept faith in Napoleon
Long after the rest of the world had given him up
For tyrant and betrayer of the revolution?
If Napoleon was like Tolstoy writing a novel
Organizing a vast army of plots and themes

Then Castro is like a poet writing an ode
(Alas that poets should be rulers
Revise that line, cut that stanza, lop off that phrase)
Paredón! Paredón!

What he did was kick out the bad men and good riddance Batista
What he is doing . . . Well, what he is trying to do is . . .
(Muse, why don't you help me with this
Are you scared of socialist experiment?)
One thing he is doing is upsetting a lot of people
Our papers are full of stories that make him out a devil
And you a fool if you like him
But they are against me too even if they don't know I exist
So let's shake, Fidel
(The hand that exists shakes the hand that doesn't)
My Fidel Castro, Star of Cuba.

III

The Hotel Teresa in Harlem is a dumpy landmark in a slum
But when Fidel Castro went there to stay
And when Nikita Khrushchev went up and hugged and kissed
him for being Mr. Wonderful
Right out in public (they get away with it, those foreigners)
Then Harlem became the capital of the world
And the true home of the united nations.

That whole bunch sitting around the hotel like in bivouac roasting chickens
And all those Negroes looking at them bug-eyed
Nobody that great ever came up there before to stay.
Of course plenty of people that great came out of Harlem
Like Jimmy Baldwin, not to mention those jazz people we all love
But the Colored that came out of Harlem like roman candles
You don't catch them going back there like a Fourth of July parade.

Now Cuba and Russia have gone to Harlem
And found it a good place for loving
That Harlem, full of rats chewing off babies' arms
And social workers trying to keep the whole place from exploding
I used to have friends up there
When I went to visit them if I passed a mirror
My whiteness would surprise me
The mind takes on darkness of skin so easily
(Of course being a Jew I'm not exactly white)
It is that easy to turn black
And then have to be in that awful boat the Negroes are in
Although it's pretty lousy being white
And having that black hatred turned on you.

What after all can a white man say but, I'm ashamed
Hey, fellas, I'm sorry . . .
Unless you are president and then you have your golden
        opportunity.
Perhaps the only thing to do is look upon each other
As two men look when they meet solitary in the deep woods
Come, black man, let us jerk off together
Like boys do to get to know each other.

Well just like others who have escaped ghettos I don't go to Harlem
        anymore
I don't like to see the trapped whom I can't set free
But when I see the big front-page photos of Castro and Khrushchev
        hugging in Harlem
A widescreen spectacle with supermen in totalscope embrace, and
        in color yet
I sit back and dig it all the way
Man it swings.

IV

BOMBS GOING OFF ALL OVER HAVANA
In Rockefeller Center the Cuban Tourist Office is closed
And across the skating rink men are putting up
The world's largest Christmas tree which will never be Christian
Even if you cut it down, make it stand on cement, decorate it with balls
It will still scream for the forest, like a wild animal
Like the gods who love freedom and topple to the saws of commerce
The gods who frighten us half to death in our dreams with their doings
And disappear when we need them most, awake.

By the time you see this, Fidel, you might not even exist anymore
My government is merciless and even now
The machine to destroy you is moving into action
The chances are you won't last long
Well so long, pal, it was nice knowing you
I can't go around with a broken heart all my life
After I got over the fall of the Spanish Republic
I guess I can get over anything
My job is just to survive.

But I wish you well, Fidel Castro
And if you do succeed in making that island
The tropic paradise God meant it to be
I'll be the first to cheer and come for a free visit if invited.

So you're not perfect, poets don't look for perfect
It's your spirit we love and the glamour of your style
I hope someday the cameras of the world
Are turned on you and me in some spot like Harlem
And then you'll get a kiss that will make Khrushchev's be forgotten
A kiss of the poet, that will make you truly good
The way you meant to be.

from *Variety Photoplays* (1967)

Curse of the Cat Woman

It sometimes happens
that the woman you meet and fall in love with
is of that strange Transylvanian people
with an affinity for cats.

You take her to a restaurant, say, or a show,
on an ordinary date, being attracted
by the glitter in her slitty eyes and her catlike walk,
and afterward of course you take her in your arms,
and she turns into a black panther
and bites you to death.

Or perhaps you are saved in the nick of time,
and she is tormented by the knowledge of her tendency:
that she daren't hug a man
unless she wants to risk clawing him up.

This puts you both in a difficult position,
panting lovers who are prevented from touching
not by bars but by circumstance:
you have terrible fights and say cruel things,
for having the hots does not give you a sweet temper.

One night you are walking down a dark street
and hear the padpad of a panther following you,
but when you turn around there are only shadows,
or perhaps one shadow too many.

You approach, calling, "Who's there?"
and it leaps on you.
Luckily you have brought along your sword,
and you stab it to death.

And before your eyes it turns into the woman you love,
her breast impaled on your sword,
her mouth dribbling blood saying she loved you
but couldn't help her tendency.

So death released her from the curse at last,
and you knew from the angelic smile on her dead face
that in spite of a life the devil owned,
love had won, and heaven pardoned her.

Frankenstein

The monster has escaped from the dungeon
where he was kept by the Baron,
who made him with knobs sticking out from each side of his neck
where the head was attached to the body
and stitching all over
where parts of cadavers were sewed together.

He is pursued by the ignorant villagers,
who think he is evil and dangerous because he is ugly
and makes ugly noises.
They wave firebrands at him and cudgels and rakes,
but he escapes and comes to the thatched cottage
of an old blind man playing on the violin Mendelssohn's "Spring Song."

Hearing him approach, the blind man welcomes him:
"Come in, my friend," and takes him by the arm.
"You must be weary," and sits him down inside the house.
For the blind man has long dreamed of having a friend
to share his lonely life.

The monster has never known kindness—the Baron was cruel,
but somehow he is able to accept it now,
and he really has no instincts to harm the old man,
for in spite of his awful looks he has a tender heart:
who knows what cadaver that part of him came from?

The old man seats him at table, offers him bread,
and says, "Eat, my friend." The monster
rears back roaring in terror.
"No, my friend, it is good. Eat—gooood,"
and the old man shows him how to eat,
and reassured, the monster eats

and says, "Eat—gooood,"
trying out the words and finding them good too.

The old man offers him a glass of wine,
"Drink, my friend. Drink—gooood."
The monster drinks, slurping horribly, and says,
"Drink—gooood" in his deep nutty voice
and smiles maybe for the first time in his life.

Then the blind man puts a cigar in the monster's mouth
and lights a large wooden match that flares up in his face.
The monster, remembering the torches of the villagers,
recoils, grunting in terror.
"No, my friend, smoke—gooood,"
and the old man demonstrates with his own cigar.
The monster takes a tentative puff
and smiles hugely, saying, "Smoke—gooood,"
and sits back like a banker, grunting and puffing.

Now the old man plays Mendelssohn's "Spring Song" on the violin
while tears come into our dear monster's eyes
as he thinks of the stones of the mob, the pleasures of mealtime,
the magic new words he has learned,
and above all of the friend he has found.

It is just as well that he is unaware,
being simple enough to believe only in the present,
that the mob will find him and pursue him
for the rest of his short unnatural life,
until trapped at the whirlpool's edge
he plunges to his death.

The Bride of Frankenstein

The Baron has decided to mate the monster,
to breed him perhaps,
in the interests of pure science, his only god.

So he goes up into his laboratory,
which he has built in the tower of the castle
to be as near the interplanetary forces as possible,
and puts together the prettiest monster-woman you ever saw,
with a body like a pinup girl
and hardly any stitching at all
where he sewed on the head of a raped and murdered beauty queen.

He sets his liquids burping, and coils blinking and buzzing,
and waits for an electric storm to send through the equipment
the spark vital for life.
The storm breaks over the castle,
and the equipment really goes crazy
like a kitchen full of modern appliances
as the lightning juice starts oozing right into that pretty corpse.

He goes to get the monster
so he will be right there when she opens her eyes,
for she might fall in love with the first thing she sees, as ducklings do.
That monster is already straining at his chains and slurping,
ready to go right to it:
he has been well prepared for coupling
by his pinching, leering keeper, who's been saying for weeks,
"Ya gonna get a little nookie, kid,"
or "How do you go for some poontang, baby?"
All the evil in him is focused on this one thing now
as he is led into her very presence.

She awakens slowly,
she bats her eyes,
she gets up out of the equipment,
and finally she stands in all her seamed glory,
a monster princess with a hairdo like a fright wig,
lightning flashing in the background
like a halo and a wedding veil,
like a photographer snapping pictures of great moments.

She stands and stares with her electric eyes,
beginning to understand that in this life too
she is just another body to be raped.

The monster is ready to go:
he roars with joy at the sight of her,
so they let him loose and he goes right for those knockers.
And she starts screaming to break your heart,
and you realize that she was just born:
in spite of her big tits she is just a baby.

But her instincts are right—
rather death than that green slobber:
she jumps off the parapet.
And then the monster's sex drive goes wild.
Thwarted, it turns to violence, demonstrating sublimation crudely,
and he wrecks the lab, those burping acids and buzzing coils,
overturning the control panel so the equipment goes off like a bomb,
and the stone castle crumbles and crashes in the storm,
destroying them all . . . perhaps.

Perhaps somehow the Baron got out of that wreckage of his dreams
with his evil intact, if not his good looks,
and more wicked than ever went on with his thrilling career.

And perhaps even the monster lived
to roam the earth, his desire still ungratified,

and lovers out walking in shadowy and deserted places
will see his shape loom up over them, their doom,
and children sleeping in their beds
wake up in the dark night screaming
as his hideous body grabs them.

Sweet Gwendolyn and the Countess

The Countess rode out on her black horse in spring
wearing her black leather riding costume.
She was scouting for disciples in the countryside
and flicked with her whip the rosebuds as she passed.

Sweet Gwendolyn in her white dress
was out gathering May flowers.
Under sunshade hat, her pale face
blushed to the singing bees,
and her golden curls lay passive on bent shoulders
as she stooped to pluck a white lily.

The Countess passing by took one look,
galloped up, and reined her stallion sharply in,
high over the modest figure
of Sweet Gwendolyn with the downcast eyes.
She leaped down from her horse and knelt,
laying the whip in tribute before the golden girl.

That foolish one swooned forward to the ground
in a great white puff of dress fabric
and a scattering of flowers. At that,
the Countess rose in all her black pride
and put her dirty leather boot hard on Gwendolyn's bent neck,
pushing down the golden head to the grass,
and gave her a smart lash across her innocently upturned behind.

Gwendolyn looked up with begging eyes
and a small whimper of submission,
as the Countess pushed her over and threw the skirt up,
exposing legs and bottom bare,

and shoved the leather whip handle between squeezed thighs of virtue,
forcing them apart to reveal the pink pulsing maidenhood.

Foolish Gwendolyn for not wearing panties.
But how could she have known what was in store?
Her skirt fell over her head like petals of a fully-opened flower,
and her legs waved in the air like stamen and pistil,
inviting the bee of the Countess's tongue
to slip in and sip nectar in the golden fuzz.

Poor Gwendolyn moaned with shame and pain
as she lay back crushing her May flowers, exposed and unresisting,
until the Countess, in full charge, pulled her to her feet,
tied the whip end around her neck,
remounted the big black horse,
and slowly trotted on,
leading the sobbing girl a captive behind her
off to her dark castle.

Whatever Happened to May Caspar?
A Narration for an Animated Cartoon

What happens to old movie stars,
those faded queens of stage and screen?
They move into hotels off Times Square maybe
where they live among their souvenirs,
near the lights, the people, the premieres
that no longer know them,
funny old ladies with hair a pink frizz,
salvaging old costumes for street clothes.

Does anyone remember May Caspar now?
She was all the rage in thirty-three
when she starred in *May Morning* with Ronald Peale,
in which she played a simple country girl
and he a prince who lost his heart among the apple blossoms.

Now thirty years later (that makes her about sixty, at least),
what does she see when she sits down to her vanity table
with its clutter of lotions?
Does she stare at the blur in the mirror
and remember how young she was in that movie,
how pure and fragile?
Before she puts on her glasses
she takes a swig out of a large perfume bottle
and goes about painting a Kewpie doll over the wreck of her face:
somehow it always comes out crooked.

Later, after her disastrous marriage to Nick Kinsella
and the divorce and the operations
(they say he beat her up horribly),
after she got back her looks,
she played femme fatale roles on divans with heavy eye makeup.

Remember *A Woman's Eyes,* with Ivan Carlovan,
in which May was the toast of Vienna
until the love of her prince turned to hate
when he discovered a stable boy was her lover
and she had to flee through snowdrifts in a sleigh
standing up behind the horses singing:
> *The heart will find a way*

but ending up in a waterfront bar in Marseilles
singing with an accordion:
> *A woman's eyes are pools of sin.*
> *Don't look too long, they'll lure you in.*

There were dozens of suicides to her record of that song.

Then came her greatest hit, *The Downward Path,*
in which she played a mature stage star
who fell in love with a young actor,
but he only used her to make it to the top
while she went downhill fast and ended in the gutter
selling flowers by the stage door
as he came out with the ingenue on his arm
and stepped into the waiting limousine.
How her beautiful eyes shone in that scene.
You knew she held no grudge, but loved him still
as she sang after him:
> *Go, beautiful youth,*
> *forget me now, for I am old.*
> *Enjoy your fame as I did mine.*

For that, America forgave her everything,
her parade of unsuitable husbands,
her drunken brawls in restaurants.
She was darling May Caspar, for a few years anyway
(her career lasted only three more years),
then she faded away.

Now forgotten, she is that funny old lady
living shabbily on a dwindling income

in a Times Square hotel, once genteel,
now full of call girls and Kansas tourists.
It gets harder and harder to pay the bills.
Back rent mounts up. Room service is cut off.
She lives on hot dogs. Her fate looks grim.
She is about to be put out in the street
with her souvenirs and wardrobe
for the winter wind to blow away,
plumes and bits of fur and photographs and dried corsages,
and she skittering after them down the streets.

But wait, here comes a late rider:
A message from the Museum of Modern Art!
They are planning a May Caspar revival,
and she is wanted to appear "in person," like the old days.
May Caspar movies stamped Authentic American Art.
She is proclaimed A Great Actress.
May Caspar Called Back to Hollywood to Make Film.
But first she goes to Last Chance,
exclusive beauty resort in Death Valley,
where they go to work on her
with hormones, vitamins, embryo implants, and surgery.

When she shows up in Hollywood her beauty is restored.
Thirty years of ravagement have been erased:
There is not a wrinkle.
Of course her strength is not what it was,
two men have to hold her up,
but she is a great trouper and the show will go on.
Today they are filming her big scene on the divan, her trademark:
Lights, Camera, Action: May Caspar acts again!

Anyway she tries, but the effort is too much for her—
the hot lights, the excitement,
her skin held taut by invisible clips,
her heart stimulated with drugs,

her head sweating under the wig,
every bit of her held together with string and sealing wax.
"Okay, Miss Caspar, give it all you've got."
The camera moves in inexorably for the close-up.
She tries desperately to think young, to hold everything up.
Those merciless lights!
Too late, it all collapses.

Good-bye, May Caspar.
We loved you
in the way we love
faithlessly.
Or are we, growing older,
ready to remember again
our great loves
of yesteryear
and go search for them
where we lost sight of them
in those shabby places,
close to the brightest
lights
that cast the deepest
shadow?

Nancy

When scolded by Aunt Fritzy Ritz
Nancy seems to lose her wits.
Nancy is very often cross
but Fritzy's the undisputed boss.
She sits in the house reading the papers
supervising Nancy's capers.

Aunt Fritzy's a peculiar sort:
she has no visible means of support.
She never seems to earn a bean
and there's no "uncle" on the scene.
The questions seem to rise a lot:
Is Fritzy Nancy's aunt, or not?
If Fritzy is related to
that awful Mrs. Meany who
Annie Rooney had to flee,
then who can Nancy really be?

Rumors are flying thick and fast;
stories from mouth to ear are passed:
"Who is Fritzy Ritz indeed
but someone overcome by greed.
Welfare pays a monthly sum
to keep that orphan in her home.
Although she looks like Etta Kett
She's older, more depraved, in debt."

One scandalous version I have heard
(of which I don't believe a word)
says Nancy's father, coming back
a little early from the track,
found his wife and Fritzy in

a most revolting act of sin.
With a knife he tried to nip
this lesbian relationship:
saw red, and stabbed; the blow went wild
and made an orphan of his child.
His wife was dead, he got the chair,
the court named Fritzy Ritz as heir.
The child, the house, the bank account
were left to Fritzy Ritz, the "aunt."

No one will make Aunt Fritzy crawl
now that she's in charge of all:
the house, the grounds, the little brat.
She'll teach her to remember that!

Poor Nancy's nature has been bent
by this negative environment.
She never will grow up at all
but stay forever three feet tall.

The Life of Joan Crawford

for Barbara Barry

She was a working girl from a small town
but the town wasn't so small
that it didn't have a railroad track
dividing the right side from the wrong side.
On the right side was the Hill,
where the swells lived in big houses,
and on the wrong side, the Hollow, where the proletariat
spent their greasy and unrewarding lives.
(For in those days the American town
was a living demonstration of Marxist theory.)

Joan of course lived in the Hollow
in one of those shacks with sagging porches
the mill put up rows of for the workers.
Her father, Tim Crawford, was the town drunk,
living on relief and odd jobs
ever since the mines closed down when Joan was a baby.
He had been waiting for them to reopen for twenty years.
Joan never knew what had happened to her mother:
Joan's birth, her mother's disappearance or death, the mine's closing,
that was in a time of violence no one would discuss.
Just mention it and her father went on a binge,
not that he was ever sober.

She sighed and went off to work in the five-and-ten
wearing her made-over dress with little washable collar and cuffs.
Even with her prole accent and the cheap bag and shoes
she was a good looker.
Men used to come by in their flashy suits and big cigars,
call her tootsie and ask for a date,
but she knew a poor girl didn't stand a chance with them.
She wasn't one of those innocents

who think a guy loves you if he gets a hard-on.
Yet she wouldn't go with any of the boys from the Hollow
because with them the future was sleazy with kids
and the ruin of her figure before she was thirty
and no fun after the honeymoon
except the Friday-night fight
when he would come home stinking, having drunk up the paycheck,
and beat her black and blue
when she threw the stack of overdue bills at him
and then screw her viciously on the dining-room table.
Some fun.
That was life in the Hollow and she wasn't having any.
She had turned down a job working in the mill,
where the pay was better but life closed like a trap on you,
and chose the more ladylike job at the five-and-ten,
where people called her Miss and she could pose genteelly
behind the Tangee cosmetic display and the ribbon counter.
For Joan had the makings of a lady
if she could ever get some dough to fix herself up with
and a speech teacher to correct her dreadful accent.

But Nature had its way with Joan at last:
spring came and handsome John Wainrich
(of the best family in town—they owned everything,
the five-and-dime, the shut mines, and the mill),
John Wainrich came in one day to collect the receipts or something
and found a million-dollar baby in his own five-and-ten-cents store.
Well, Joan fell hard
and went out with him in his big car,
and of course in the moonlight she let him have his way with her.
She used to meet him on the sly
when he could get away from the country club
and the milk-white debutante he was engaged to,
and they would drive out to roadhouses
where he wouldn't be seen by his swell friends.
Joan had pride,

but what is a woman's pride when she's in love.
What it came to, a few months later,
was that she got pregnant,
and just as she was about to break the good news,
he told her he was going to be married
and would have to stop seeing her until after the wedding,
that it was just a marriage of convenience
and wouldn't make any difference to them.
So she couldn't tell him then—she would have died first.

My Great Love, she muttered sarcastically,
he didn't even use a scumbag.
And she went off to the city,
where she got a job as receptionist in an office.
Her boss, Mr. Harris, was an older but dignified man
with a wife at home on Park Avenue, the victim of neurosis and wealth—
with all that money she could buy neither health nor happiness.
Joan used to listen to Mr. Harris's troubles
when she brought him his Alka-Seltzer mornings.
And when she was promoted to secretary, they would have dinner out,
and she'd advise him on business,
she being a girl with a good head on her shoulders.

In Mr. Harris's company she saw the world and learned fast.
She lost her small-town look and learned to dress,
wearing hat and gloves, to fluff out her hair
and drink vermouth cocktails.
And while retaining the colorful idiom of the Hollow,
her grammar improved and her voice lost its nasal whine.
Joan was a knockout in every way,
from honest eyes and square shoulders
to the narrow hips of a tango dancer.

Nothing showed yet in the baby department.
At night Joan looked critically at herself in the mirror:
not a bulge, but baby was in there all right,
and her eyes went bitter as she thought of its father,

her great love, hmph.
"Well, young feller, at least we'll have each other.
But I'd better be making preparations.
A working girl can't leave things to the caterer."

Then her boss proposed: he'd divorce his wife and marry her.
"Gee, Mr. Harris. I think you're swell but I can't.
There is a real big favor you could do for me, though,"
and she told him how she gave her all for love
and her lover turned out to be a louse.
So Mr. Harris set her up in a little flat until the baby came.
He didn't make any demands on her or anything,
not yet, anyway: it was sort of a promissory note
to be paid off later when she grew to love him out of gratitude.

But her ex-lover, John Wainrich, came to town
with his new wedding ring on and tracked her down,
and misunderstanding the arrangement, called her a few names
but swore she was his and he'd never give her up.
Joan still loved him but had the courage
to flee to a cheap hotel.
She got a job as dance-hall hostess, dime-a-dance,
six months pregnant, but with a brave smile
as the customers stepped on her toes.
They found her a good Joe and a willing ear
as they told her their troubles
while rubbing off against her to a slow fox trot.

One of her customers, impressed by her dancing,
got her to enter a dance marathon with him for prize money—
she needed that dough for the little stranger—
but the strain was too much for her,
marathon-dancing in her seventh month!

She came to on a hospital bed
with no makeup on and a white cloth over her forehead like a nun
to see her griddle-faced father looking down on her,

his mouth boozy as ever, but in his heart
vowing to go on the wagon if God would spare her life:
"Come home with me, Joanie, I'll take care of you."
"And baby too, papa?"
"Didn't they tell you, Joanie? The baby . . ."
"Oh, no. . . ."
And tears of mourning still in her eyes
she went back home to the Hollow and kept house for her father.

She had two visits shortly after returning home:
First, John's pale bride came by, big with child,
neglect driving her to seek out her rival.
When she saw Joan so sweet and good
instead of some tramp home-wrecker type,
she burst into tears and confessed she knew John didn't love her
but hoped he would when the baby was born, his heir.
The bitterness in Joan's heart turned to pity—
weren't they both women who had suffered?—
so she forgave her and they wept together:
Joan never could resist being a pal.

The other visit was from old Mr. Wainrich, John's father.
(Never had the Hollow seen so many long cars drive through.)
The old capitalist had a confession to make:
"When I saw you at the window watering the geraniums
I could have sworn you were your mother."
"You knew my mother, Mr. Wainrich?" asked Joan astonished.
"Yes. Bette wasn't like the other women in the Hollow.
She was a Davis you know. Her parents
had been plantation people down in Georgia,
and even if they did end up here in the Hollow
she never forgot that she was a thoroughbred."
"Are you trying to tell me that you loved my mother?" Joan gasped.

"Yes, I loved her, but the heir to an industrial empire
isn't free to marry whom he chooses,

so my family chose an appropriate bride for me.
At that time I was running our coal mines here,
where Tim Crawford worked.
He was the biggest and toughest man in the Hollow,
so naturally he was spokesman for the boys.
He had loved your mother for years,
but she knew what it meant for a woman to marry a miner
and live in constant fear of a cave-in.
And she hated his coarse language and crude manners: she was a lady.
And besides, she loved me.
But when I broke the news of my engagement to her
(I explained it was just a marriage of convenience
and it wouldn't make any difference to us)
she married Tim just to spite me.
But it wasn't enough for her: right on my wedding day
she got Tim Crawford to call the men out on strike,
and, with violence surging around the Hill,
I had the biggest wedding ever seen in these parts.
I was coal and my bride was steel: what a merger!
The president came, and there were reporters from Chicago,
and your mother, already big with child, leading a picket line.

That strike went on for months, and you were born in the middle of it.
But we couldn't go on apart, your mother and I.
We knew we were sinners, but we managed to meet on the sly,
although the strike had turned the town into a battlefield
and we belonged to opposing armies.
Finally we decided to run away together, but just at that time
a load of scabs I was importing to work the mines arrived,
and there was a tremendous battle between them and the miners,
led by Tim Crawford of course.
The miners had lead pipes and dynamite,
but we had the National Guard in full battle dress.
Your mother and I, eloping, got caught in the middle
and took refuge in a deserted mine,
and I don't know which side did it, but a stick of dynamite

was thrown down the shaft, and your mother
was buried by a ton of falling rock."
(Joan moaned and hid her face in her hands.)
"It was useless to do anything so I left her there.
Why say anything when no one knew?
She was destroyed by the strike she had started.
The mines were shut down for good of course,
I couldn't bear the memory.
They would have had to be shut anyway,
we were losing money on them."
"And that's why daddy never knew what happened to mother,
raising me all by himself, and took to drink . . ."
"Yes, and I went back home to my wife and our little John was born
and I tried to forget . . ."
"Promise me one thing, Mr. Wainrich," Joan said,
"for the sake of my mother's memory,
that you'll open the mines again and give daddy back his old job."

Joan had a lot to think about in the days that followed.
One day she got a call to come up right away to the big house
and, arriving, found John's wife dying,
having given birth to a child, and asking for her.
The pale bride lay holding her child, the Wainrich heir,
but seeing Joan, she sat up with her last strength and said,
"I give him to you" and fell back dead.
Joan fainted away, and when she came to,
it seemed a long time later, after the funeral and the mourning,
John Wainrich held her in his arms and was saying over and over,
"I am yours now, she gave me to you."
"But she meant the child," Joan cried.
"Both of us are yours, my darling."

So Joan found her place in life at last.
They always said she'd make it up there, surrounded by the help,
a lady, moving gracefully among the guests.
And what a difference now:

the miners in tuxes standing around the punch bowl with the swells,
the colored butler joining in the fun with loud yaks,
a new era, the classless society,
brought about by the smartest little woman in the U.S.A.,
Ladies and Gentlemen: Miss Joan Crawford.

World War II

It was over Target Berlin the flak shot up our plane
just as we were dumping bombs on the already smoking city
on signal from the lead bomber in the squadron.
The plane jumped again and again as the shells burst under us,
sending jagged pieces of steel rattling through our fuselage.
It was pure chance
that none of us got ripped by those fragments.

Then, being hit, we had to drop out of formation right away,
losing speed and altitude,
and when I figured out our course with trembling hands on the
        instruments
(I was navigator)
we set out on the long trip home to England
alone, with two of our four engines gone
and gas streaming out of holes in the wing tanks.
That morning at briefing
we had been warned not to go to nearby Poland,
partly liberated then by the Russians,
although later we learned that another crew in trouble
had landed there anyway,
and patching up their plane somehow,
returned gradually to England
roundabout by way of Turkey and North Africa.
But we chose England, and luckily
the Germans had no fighters to send up after us then,
for this was just before they developed their jet.
To lighten our load we threw out
guns and ammunition, my navigation books, all the junk,
and made it over Holland
with a few good-bye fireworks from the shore guns.

Over the North Sea the third engine gave out
and we dropped low over the water.
The gas gauge read empty, but by keeping the nose down
a little gas at the bottom of the tank sloshed forward
and kept our single engine going.
High overhead, the squadrons were flying home in formation
—the raids had gone on for hours after us.
Did they see us down there in our trouble?
We radioed our final position for help to come
but had no idea if anyone
happened to be tuned in and heard us,
and we crouched together on the floor,
knees drawn up and head down
in regulation position for ditching,
listened as the engine stopped, a terrible silence,
and we went down into the sea with a crash,
just like hitting a brick wall,
jarring bones, teeth, eyeballs panicky.
Who would ever think water could be so hard?
You black out, and then come to
with water rushing in like a sinking-ship movie.

All ten of us started getting out of there fast:
there was a convenient door in the roof to climb out by,
one at a time. We stood in line,
water up to our thighs and rising.
The plane was supposed to float for twenty minutes,
but with all those flak holes
who could say how long it really would?
The two life rafts popped out of the sides into the water,
but one of them only half inflated,
and the other couldn't hold everyone,
although they all piled into it, except the pilot,
who got into the limp raft that just floated.
The radio operator and I, out last,
(Did that mean we were least aggressive, least likely to survive?)

we stood on the wing watching the two rafts
being swept off by waves in different directions.
We had to swim for it.
Later they said the cords holding rafts to plane
broke by themselves, but I wouldn't have blamed them
for cutting them loose, for fear
that by waiting the plane would go down
and drag them with it.

I headed for the overcrowded good raft
and after a clumsy swim in soaked heavy flying clothes
got there and hung onto the side.
The radio operator went for the half-inflated raft
where the pilot lay with water sloshing over him,
but he couldn't swim, even with his life vest on.
Being from the Great Plains,
his strong farmer's body didn't know
how to wallow through the water properly,
and a wild current seemed to sweep him farther off.
One minute we saw him on top of a swell
and perhaps we glanced away for a minute
but when we looked again he was gone
just as the plane went down sometime around then
when nobody was looking.

It was midwinter and the waves were mountains
and the water ice water.
You could live in it twenty-five minutes,
the Ditching Survival Manual said.
Since most of the crew were squeezed on my raft
I had to stay in the water hanging on.
My raft? It was their raft—they got there first so they would live.
Twenty-five minutes I had.
Live, live, I said to myself.
You've got to live.
There looked like plenty of room on the raft

from where I was and I said so,
but they said no.

When I figured the twenty-five minutes were about up
and I was getting numb,
I said I couldn't hold on anymore,
and a little rat-faced boy from Alabama, one of the gunners,
got into the icy water in my place,
and I got on the raft in his.
He insisted on taking off his flying clothes,
which was a fatal mistake because even wet clothes are protection,
and then worked hard, kicking with his legs, and we all paddled,
to get to the other raft,
and we tied them together.
The gunner got in the raft with the pilot
and lay in the wet.
Shortly after, the pilot started gurgling green foam from his mouth—
maybe he was injured in the crash against the instruments—
and by the time we were rescued,
he and the little gunner were both dead.

That boy who took my place in the water,
who died instead of me,
I don't remember his name even.
It was like those who survived the death camps
by letting others go into the ovens in their place.
It was him or me, and I made up my mind to live.
I'm a good swimmer,
but I didn't swim off in that scary sea
looking for the radio operator when he was washed away.
I suppose, then, once and for all,
I chose to live rather than be a hero, as I still do today,
although at that time I believed in being heroic, in saving the world,
even if, when opportunity knocked,
I instinctively chose survival.

As evening fell the waves calmed down
and we spotted a boat, far off, and signaled with a flare gun,
hoping it was English not German.
The only two who cried on being found
were me and a gunner, the other gay member of the crew.
The rest kept straight faces.

It was a British air-sea rescue boat:
they hoisted us up on deck,
dried off the living and gave us whiskey and put us to bed,
and rolled the dead up in blankets,
and delivered us all to a hospital on shore
for treatment or disposal.

This was a minor accident of war:
two weeks in a rest camp at Southport on the Irish Sea
and we were back at Grafton-Underwood, our base,
ready for combat again,
the dead crewmen replaced by living ones,
and went on hauling bombs over the continent of Europe,
destroying the Germans and their cities.

Giant Pacific Octopus

I live with a Giant Pacific Octopus:
he settles himself down beside me on the couch in the evening.
With two arms he holds a book
that he reads with his single eye:
he wears a pair of glasses over it for reading.

Two more arms go walking over to the sideboard across the room
where the crackers and cheese spread he loves are,
and they send back endless canapés, like a conveyor belt.

While his mouth is drooling and chomping,
another arm comes over and gropes me lightly:
it is like a breeze on my balls, that sweet tentacle.

Other arms start slipping around my body under my clothes,
they wiggle right in, one around my waist,
and all over, and down the crack of my ass.

I am drawn into his midst where his hot mouth waits for kisses,
and I kiss him and make him into a boy
as all Giant Pacific Octopuses are really
when you take them into your arms.

All their arms fluttering around you
become everywhere sensations of pleasure.
So, his sweet eye looks at me and his little mouth kisses me
and I swear he has the body of a Greek god,
my Giant Pacific Octopus boychik.

So this was what was in store
when I first saw him in the aquarium
huddled miserably on the rock

ignoring the feast of live crabs
they put in his windowed swimming pool.

You take home a creature like that, who needs love,
who is a mess when you meet
but who can open up like a flower with petal arms waving around—
    a beauty—
and it is a total pleasure to have him around,
even collapsible as he is like a big toy,
for as long as he will stay, one night or a lifetime,
for as long as god will let you have him.

Tailspin

Going into a tailspin
in those days meant curtains.
No matter how hard you pulled back on the stick
the nose of the plane wouldn't come up.

Spinning round, headed for a target of earth,
the whine of death in the wing struts,
instinct made you try to pull out of it that way, by force,
and for years aviators spiraled down and crashed.

Who could have dreamed that the solution
to this dreaded aeronautical problem
was so simple?
Every student flier learns this nowadays:
you move the joystick in the direction of the spin,
and like a miracle the plane stops turning
and you are in control again
to pull the nose up out of the dive.

In panic we want to push the stick away from the spin,
wrestle the plane out of it,
but the trick is, as in everything,
to go with the turning willingly,
rather than fight—give in, go with it,
and that way come out of your tailspin whole.

from *A Full Heart* (1973)

New York

I live in a beautiful place, a city
people claim to be astonished
when you say you live there.
They talk of junkies, muggings, dirt, and noise,
missing the point completely.
I tell them where they live it is hell,
a land of frozen people.
They never think of people.

Home, I am astonished by this environment
that is also a form of nature
like those paradises of trees and grass,
but this is a people paradise,
where we are the creatures mostly,
though thank God for dogs, cats, sparrows, and roaches.
This vertical place is no more an accident
than the Himalayas are.
The city needs all those tall buildings
to contain the tremendous energy here.
The landscape is in a state of balance.
We do God's will whether we know it or not:
where I live the streets end in a river of sunlight.

Nowhere else in the country do people
show just what they feel—
we don't put on any act.
Look at the way New Yorkers
walk down the street. It says,
I don't care. What nerve,
to dare to live their dreams, or nightmares,
and no one bothers to look.

True, you have to be an expert to live here.
Part of the trick is not to go anywhere, lounge about,
go slowly in the midst of the rush for novelty.
Anyway, besides the eats the big event here
is the streets, which are full of love—
we hug and kiss a lot. You can't say that
for anywhere else around. For some
it's a carnival of sex—
there's all the opportunity in the world.
For me it is no different:
out walking, my soul seeks its food.
It knows what it wants.
Instantly it recognizes its mate, our eyes meet,
and our beings exchange a vital energy,
the universe goes on Charge,
and we pass by without holding.

Being Jewish

My mother's family was made up of loving women.
They were, on the whole, bearers,
though Esther, the rich sister, had only one,
she was the exception.

Sarah, the oldest, had five with her first husband
(that was still in Poland),
was widowed and came here,
where she married a man with four of his own,
and together they had another five,
all of whom she raised, feeding them in relays,
except little Tillie, who sat in the kitchen
and ate with everyone, meaning all the time,
resulting in a fat figure
that made her despair of ever finding a husband,
but miraculously she did,
for God has decreed there is someone for everyone,
if you're desperate enough
and will take what you can get.

Aunt Rachel had twelve, raising them in a stable.
She was married to a junk dealer
who kept horses to haul the wagons.
He was famous for his stinginess,
so they lived in a shack surrounded by bales of hay.
That was in America, in a slum called Bronzeville
that the black people have now inherited from the Jews,
God help them.
Then, as now, plenty of kids turned out bad,
going to work for that Jewish firm, Murder Incorporated,
or becoming junkies like one of my cousins did.
My mother only had six

but that's not counting. . . I'll say no more
than she was always pregnant,
with a fatalistic "What can you do?"
("Plenty," her friend Blanche replied—she was liberated.
"You don't have to breed like a rabbit.")
Like her mother who had a baby a year in Poland
until Grandpa left for America,
giving her a rest.
There were women who kept bearing
even then, mysteriously, as from habit.

Women were always tired in those days and no wonder,
with the broken-down bodies they had
and their guts collapsed,
for with every child they got a dragging down.
My mother finally had hers
tied back up in the hospital, and at the same time
they tied those over-fertile tubes,
which freed her from "God's terrible curse on women."

And not just the bearing, but the work:
the pots couldn't be big enough for those hungry broods—
Sarah used hospital pots for hers.
And then the problem of filling the pots,
getting up at dawn to go to the fishing boats
for huge fish carcasses cheap,
buying bushels of half-spoiled vegetables for pennies,
begging the butcher for bones,
and then lugging it all home on their bad legs.
They didn't think of their looks for a minute,
and better they didn't, shapeless as that life made them.
(And yet they remained attractive to their men,
by the evidence of their repeated pregnancies.)
They just went around wrecks, always depressed,
unable to cope, or hiding in bed
while the children screamed.

"Escape, escape, there must be escape"
was my mother's theme song, until at last
her children escaped from her and her misery,
having wrecked her life, that endless sacrifice,
for what?

I see the proletarian women like them on the streets,
cows with udders to the waist
lugging black oilcloth shopping bags,
the *mamale*s, the *mamacita*s, the mammies,
the breeders of the world with loving eyes.
They sit around the kitchen table with full hearts,
telling each other their troubles—
never enough money, the beasts their men were to them,
how Leo hit Esther in the face on the street,
the sorrow life was for a woman, a mother,
the children turning out no good—
and fed each other pieces of leftover meat from the icebox
to make up a little for life's pain
and sighing, drank tea
and ate good bread and butter.

The Lost, Dancing

after Cavafy

When the drums come to your door
do not try to shut them out,
do not turn away and resist them,
for they have come to tell you what you need to hear.
They are your fate.
When Antony heard them
he knew then that he had lost Egypt forever.
He did not shriek or tear his clothes
for he always knew they would come someday.
What the drums speak to you
is so inevitable you have to agree with them—
nothing else could be right.
So when the drummers and dancers come to your door
your life changes,
and with no bitterness
but with a sad smile
—after all, what you had you had,
you loved the way few men love—
and as someone who was worthy of such a kingdom,
join the army of the lost, dancing,
follow the drums
and turn and wave good-bye
to the Alexandria you are losing.

Carnival, Rio de Janeiro, 1974

David's Dream

You're not ready for the convent yet.

—David Del Tredici

He said that he dreamed
that everyone was meeting at the baths tonight
except me.
I'll be teaching there in the morning
so I couldn't go.

Well, he's got my number all right, I'm no fun.
I talk liberation
but my actions show otherwise,
and he dreams me as I really am,
a ruler-snapping nun
keeping the class in line.

My image is definitely bad.

I only show up at the baths
when morning guilt lights up the shabby linoleum
and the employees are scrubbing the love juice
off the walls and ceilings of the orgy room,
and the customers are putting on their jeans
anxious to go home.

That's when I arrive with my attendance book
and a sad sack stuffed with experience,
teaching what I don't believe in
and nobody wants to hear.

THE LESSON
*If all you can do is teach
don't do it at the baths.*

If you go to the baths
don't go in the morning.
And if you go into the steam room
take off your habit, baby,
and leave your ruler home.

Sharks

Especially at evening
everyone knows the sharks come in
when the sun makes puddles of blood on the sea
and the shadows darken.

It is then, as night comes on,
the sharks of deep water
approach the shore
and beware, beware, the late swimmer.

from *Stars in My Eyes* (1978)

Mae West

She comes on drenched in a perfume called Self-Satisfaction
from feather boa to silver pumps.

She does not need to be loved by you,
though she'll give you credit for good taste.
Just because you say you love her
she's not throwing herself at your feet in gratitude.

Every other star reveals how worthless she feels
by crying when the hero says, Marry me,
or how unhoped-for the approval is
when the audience applauds her big number,
but Mae West takes it as her due:
she knows she's good.

She expects the best for her self
and knows she's worth what she costs,
and she costs plenty—
she's not giving anything away.

She enjoys her admirers, fat daddy or muscleman,
and doesn't confuse vanity and sex,
though she never turns down pleasure,
lapping it up.

Above all she enjoys her self,
swinging her body that says, Me, me, me, me.
Why not have a good time?
As long as you amuse me, go on,
I like you slobbering over my hand, big boy,
I have a right to.

Most convincing, we know all this
not by her preaching
but by her presence—it's no act.
Every word and look and movement
spells Independence:
she likes being herself.

And we who don't
can only look on, astonished.

Comeback

It's not a comeback. I refuse to use that word. It's a return.

—Norma Desmond, in *Sunset Boulevard*

A limousine pulled up to Paradise Pictures,
and a heavily veiled woman stepped out.
The studio guard hurried to open the great doors,
and she swept in with a whispering of furs
straight through the ranks of secretaries
to the center of the hive
where T.L., top man at Paradise,
sat at his fabulous round desk with the sword hanging over it,
which he claimed symbolized his expendability
but was said to be used on all rivals for his job.

Connie Comeback! he exclaimed, rising,
and came forward to take her warmly by both hands
and bring her into the heartland.
Why haven't we seen you in all these years?
Connie settled herself in a spider-web chair,
pushed back her veils to reveal
the still-famous face lacquer perfect,
and lit a gold-tipped Fatima.
You haven't changed a bit, Connie, said T.L.
with genuine awe like before the Lincoln Memorial.

Haven't I, T.L.? She blew out a passionate cloud of smoke.
Then give me a picture. I'm ready to work again.
I was always good box office, wasn't I?

Number one B.O., Connie,
you packed them in and made millions for us but . . .
The telephone interrupted him.

It was the great Vosberg, the director,
who was dedicating his life to Connie
although she had divorced him and gone on to six more husbands.
His tireless care alone kept her alive
for her compulsive rituals of beautification.
If Vosberg had once dreamed they would come out of retirement
that hope was long since dead: she was a lost cause.
But he knew that if she ever realized she was a has-been
her glass brain would shatter forever.

At the peak of her career, Connie Comeback, called Countess by friends,
went into complete retirement.
They had been filming *Daylight Hours*,
in which she played the daytime mistress of a man
who had to stay home nights with his invalid wife.
The ingenue, Monica Moaner, playing the nothing role
of the man's secretary, stole every scene
with the wiggle of her young young body,
so Connie, impulsively, attacked her with a blowtorch.

It was doing Monica a favor really
because her face wasn't star material and this way plastic surgery
could create for her the perfect face she needed for her career.

Connie disappeared under heavy sedation,
and Monica rose to fame and fortune in *Daylight Hours*,
though now she too was box office poison
and had joined the mah-jongg set in a bungalow colony
waiting for the call from the studio that never came.

Sorry T.L., Vosberg was saying
in his heavy accent from the car phone,
she insisted on me driving her out to the studio
—I couldn't keep her home—
so string her along, will you?
Tell her you'll put her in a picture again, anything,

just keep her happy.
Tomorrow I'll tell her it was all a dream.
I've got her medicine ready:
as he spoke, he took a full cocktail shaker of martinis
out of the liquor cabinet built into the glove compartment
and dropped a knockout pill into it.

As T.L. hung up and thoughtfully turned back
to his famous visitor Connie was saying,
I've found the perfect vehicle for my comeback,
and she produced a bulky manuscript from beneath her furs.
It's the story of a hillbilly girl
who is found by a psychiatrist on vacation in the woods.
He analyzes her for fun,
and she becomes the leading international hostess
on the Washington political scene,
all the while secretly supporting
a bunch of half-wit relations in the cellar and attic.
You get the point? They can't change your soul!

Countess, you always come up with sure-fire ideas.
We really miss you here at the studio.
The new ones, they don't have glamour anymore.
(T.L. grew expansive with his wisdom.)
Hollywood is not a place, or even an industry.
It's the heart of America,
and you're still enthroned there as queen.

You mean you want me back, T.L.?

Back, hell. Countess, you've never been away.
The boys on the lot still talk about you,
and if the technicians respect a star, she's a real star.
And T.L. picked up a microphone,
switching off the loudspeaker system under his desk,
and with a tremor in his voice and real tears in his eyes announced

that Connie Comeback would make her comeback
in *The Upstairs and Downstairs of the Heart.*
If the best seller shook the nation
the movie would go off like an atomic bomb!

He pressed a button and flashbulbs popped around them
while from a loudspeaker came applause and cheers.
Tears of gratitude rolled darkly down Connie's cheeks.
They still wanted her. . . . they wanted her back. . . .
She straightened up proudly: Hell, she'd never been away!

Then like a liner guided from the dock by tugboats
and salutes from shore guns and crowds and flags
Connie Comeback leaned back in her long limousine
waving a gloved hand at her millions of fans
and left the studio sipping
her cocktail of forgetfulness.

from *New and Selected Poems,*

from the Book of My Life (1987)

Triad

A temple sculpture: Two Warriors in Combat.
Down between their knees a Female
with one of their stone pricks up her cunt,
at the same time, bending over backward
to take the other's cock in her mouth,
while the men cross swords above her.

Even confronting each other with sharp steel,
according to this ancient mystery
something tender bridges them,
a goddess joining the warriors in her body,
for she has to be a goddess
and this is obviously her function:
but is she consoling, neutralizing,
trying to bring peace about,
or delivering the charge that sets the swords a-clashing?

Or do they only appear to fight
to deny the sexual connection below?
But no one seems to be hiding anything—
it's open as a diagram, illustrative,
rather than a daisy chain like The Three Graces.

When we say men are "joined" in battle,
do we too mean like this,
opposition at one pole, concord at the other,
and in the contest both at once?
Beyond the fierce worldly display,
the glitter of rivalry, the squiring of women—
a secret brotherhood?

And this goddess created out of a mutual need?
As if maleness cannot mate without a medium:
it's within the female principle, men unite—or fight!

Oh, Brother!

1.

When you look, fierce face, in the mirror mornings
is it absolutely necessary to groan?
It's not that you're ugly really, just old and ravaged
with, wouldn't you say, haunted eyes?
Well, you alone know what they've seen.

If your life has turned you into this, remember,
you've worked hard not to make it even worse.
Think of all the talking and screaming therapies you've tried,
not to mention acupuncture, diet cures, years of yoga exercises,
and, as good as anything really, prayer.

Instead of hating your face, *shmeggege*,
can't you dredge up the least compassion
for what you've gone through? Tenderness, perhaps?
Don't scorn yourself. Give yourself a medal, pops.
It's been a long haul out of the pits,
if you are out yet,

and you look it!

2.

It's in the bathroom that I loudly groan
over my incandescent foolishness—

when I think of what I've said and done,
especially tonight at the dinner table.

O why did I have to blab like that
among those grownup people?

You are a jerk and never will be other,
and right thou art to know thy estimate—
      it's written all over your silly face,

and therefore you may well invoke
the eternal fraternal principle,

a cry resounding down the ages
to gods and man alike,
      from Job to Christ-on-the-Cross to you:

O BROTHER!

From Poland

"After soulless Germany," my sister writes,
"to be in an absolutely soulful land . . .
the złoty not buying much
even if there were anything to buy . . .
the bureaucracy frightening, but everyone used to it,
patiently standing on line . . .
sweet and helpful and unspoiled."
Reading that, I think I could live there
on bread and potatoes.

Ma said that from Lamaz, her village,
Warsaw was a two-day trip by horse and wagon.
My sister writes that now
"it's an hour by superhighway. . . .

"Some old houses are still there. . . . a countrywoman
came out of one,
we just stood staring at each other, me in western clothes,
my passport full of border stamps. . . .
her daughter in the background
wearing torn leggings and a quilted vest.
Inside, just a little room
with a porcelain stove in the corner
and a bunk on each wall. . . . onion skins
on the floor of boards and dirt—
cozy enough to move into at once."

Ma always said her brother, Jake, the favorite,
got to sleep on top of the stove.
She slept in the rafters with the chickens
and the barrel of herring and sack of groats to last the winter.
They called her little pig, she was so fat,

too slow for blackberrying when her sister went at dawn—
Esther yelled at her for trying to follow,
Esther, the smart one, who learned to read and write
and kept in touch with their father in America.
He was a tinsmith and when he worked on the church roof
drank with the priest. But then, he was half-goy,
the child of his mother's love affair with a Polish landowner.
Ma told it proudly, the old scandal, but lowered her voice
to explain why she herself was always taken for Christian.
Grandma was from prosperous Jews with a farm
who never approved of the big, fair-haired tinsmith,
so they eloped to poor little Lamaz,
where people lined up to read the only newspaper.

"I kept my father's photograph until we got to America," Ma said,
"and I was so happy to see him at the dock,
but when I picked up a pretty candy box in the gutter
in wonder at such a treasure being thrown away,
he smacked me across the face and called me dumbbell.
That night I tore his picture up.
I was only happy in Lamaz."
"Did I ever tell you," she tells me again, "how the milk
turned sour in the pail and we drank it that way?"
"There were no demands on me there," she says,
an old woman in Florida now, her children grown and gone.
"I didn't have to do anything. I could sit
eating my bowl of kasha all day long."

My sister writes: "We asked the oldest people in town
about the Jews. . . . None left, they told me, vaguely,
the Nazi time was the end of them, and showed me
where the Jewish cemetery had been,
a grassy area with trees, fenced in."

Narcissus

The way I felt about myself for so long—
just another pretty face the world adored,
not in the least corresponding to the real me—
that seeing my reflection in the holy pool
I had journeyed far for and filled with my tears,
was a shocker, but frankly, what a relief
to confront the truth at last
in waters uninterested in pretty,
a depth analysis as it were.

For once feeling if not love, then tolerance,
if not approval, sympathy then,
I started treating that reflected creature better—
feeding him, caressing the high-hunched shoulders,
the tortured brow and caved-in chest,
the cold, orphaned genitals,
all so unloved-looking and neglected.
None of it had belonged to me before.

Unwanted Forever, the message in the sibylline waters:
no feeding, no caresses, will ever comfort the pain
or calm those giant fears of a child
who still needs more love than anyone can give
and who will never grow up or learn anything more,
but, as the magic pool showed me, is mine
and mine to care for.

Poems on a Theme

In Praise

The discharges of the body
are wonderful and numerous:
snot and come and spit,
the yellow stream of pee,
sweat and tears and mucus,
but best of all is shit.

Let's take another look at it.

＊

Who but me will celebrate
the bathroom and the running water,
the ball that floats in the toilet tank
and on older ones a pull-chain,
the hair-trap in the shower drain,
the tiles of purest porcelain,
the cabinet of fluffy towels,
and so we can be blissfully alone
with the movement of our bowels,
with our assholes and our cocks—
a bathroom door that locks.

＊

My shitting machine has a mind of its own:
I think of it as the sport of an off-year
like that Willys manufactured just one season and no one bought
except a schmuck who went around lamenting
he got a lemon, parts dropping all over the road,
until far from the garage and insurance expired,
the rear end fell out.

＊

Testing the possibility that knowledge
might enter when the sphincter is relaxed
(don't they say bowel training in infancy
destroys the natural aptitude for learning?),
I taped on the toilet wall
a list of Japanese words and phrases,
reading them over every time
I sat down on the can,
preparing for a vacation in Japan.

The theory didn't work, though:
not a word sank in with the outward flow,
and I didn't go.

＊

It is crucial to follow the impulse
even if the bathroom is down the hall
or, worse, beside the living room,
as it always is when you're a guest
and everyone is out there at the table
having breakfast.

It is so easy to put off,
especially when the feeling's
Can I? Should I? Dare I try?
risking a weekend of constipation
and farting, with difficulty silenced.
Next morning is another chance,
though no guarantee, even with lots of coffee
for stimulation.

A strange house, toilet shared,
maids chatting, people rattling the knob,
anything can inhibit. Somehow
the vow must be taken to do it anyhow,

as if your mother had greeted it
with joy when you did it in your pants
or on the floor instead of in the nappy—
how she shrieked at the messy pile.
Odd that we expected her to smile. . . .
Are we still trying
not to make her unhappy?

＊

Did you hear the splash?
the boy next door would ask
as I perched embarrassed
on the cold rim of the tub
and he sat on the can.

Praise Jesus, always cried
an elderly colored man
when he was done,
commemorated likewise
by religious Jews and rabbis,
regular in praise
of their Almighty One.

＊

Shy Guy

Such a dear fellow, such a shy one,
doing his job but never praised for it,
dug at, scratched, and harshly wiped,
either ignored in public
or joked about.
Put yourself in his place:
how do you feel
when somebody calls you an asshole?

The face gets endless care and beautifying,
and though he's dying to be glamorous too,
nobody uses makeup on him.
The hair is brushed and dressed,
the hands caressed,
the eyes looked deeply into,
and even the cunt . . . a man I know
claims he can stare at a cunt for hours—
but who wants to gaze up an asshole?

Frustrated in his longing
for, if not public recognition,
at least appreciation, do you blame him,
ordered to squeeze himself tight
and not let out a peep for hours,
for dropping a loud one
in the middle of a cocktail party
or your big romantic moment?

We take his cooperation for granted,
and then it's all his fault, when sore with piles
or sullen in constipation,
he soon learns he gets plenty of attention,
though not the kind he craves:
we throw up our hands and submit him
to the harsh spotlight of medical procedures
or, worse, the surgical amphitheatre,

never imagining what's wrong is us,
for identifying him with the shit
he so elegantly expels.

Afghanistan

Once you've been stranded in desert
you love all wetness,
the splashing of fountains at sundown in dusty plazas,
even the banal dribble of faucets,
become total pleasure.

When your ramshackle bus breaks down on a remote plain
you wait and wait, squatting in its shadow
with the robed and veiled, the more patient ones than you.
You try to take comfort from
the barren sweep of mountain ahead
and the nomad encampment visible on a far slope, as stony as this one.
The ear is assailed by a buzz of insects,
perhaps around a patch of stiff, staring-eyed sunflowers
rattled by gusts.
Something grew them there, surely,
but long ago.

No water is wet enough
to irrigate the thirst that grows here now,
though Pepsi-Cola, if there was any, would be ambrosia.
But, the ancients say,
better not drink in heat of day—wait for sundown.
Still, the imagination goes desolate,
pictures thirst-crazed lost staggerers
after illusory lakes on false horizons.

Hours, or is it days, of this,
and when you can't stand it anymore, the first change occurs,
like a shift in bedrock, a settling of the floor—
you accept being stuck there.
One place is as good as another, so why not here?

Someone begins playing a wild jangle of music,
and there is even a breeze.

It is then that rescue comes, a truck
crowded with molten-eyed men in rakish turbans,
and you climb up onto piles of bags in back
full of some scratchy harvest of wool or wheat,
and after an hour of bumping over a stony track
the mud walls greet you of an oasis town
where intense gardens enclose pomegranate trees
at once in fruit and flower.

And finally in a caravanserai-hotel
where the men settle down cross-legged with pots of tea
on rug-draped divans in the gloom
comes the ultimate, soul-drenching blessing in the desert world,
the world of the ancestors, of the old power:

in your room you strip off dust-caked clothes
down to tender skin, pores open to everything now,
and turn on the shower.

To Love

Away from home on a tour in the West
I worried about you constantly, my dearest,
until I had a dream one night where you
were a large plant I was chopping down with a shovel:
first I slashed off your feet
and then battered your head in, that head
that has already been attacked
by scalpel, drill, and saw
and is always blindly bumping things,
making my heart ache.

I woke in a sweat of course,
but after the shock wore away that I
could do such a thing to you, my angel, even in a dream,
I saw how absolutely necessary it was—
your needs had pursued me across a continent,
and this was the only way of getting free, of renouncing
even for a week the relentless care of you,
the concern of my days and nights: how to keep you,
an exotic, delicate plant, alive in an arctic clime,
though in my dream, I must admit,
you were a vigorous weed, bigger than me.

And then, my leafy, my green one,
whom I water daily and put in the sun,
after chopping you down and shoveling you away
I could leave you in God's hands,
and, loving you not the less for being free,
went almost lighthearted on with my journey.

from *Counting Myself Lucky,*

Poems 1963–1992 (1992)

The Winners and the Losers

I stood before them
and told them of my life,
the sorrows and the losses—
in short, the human condition.

I could see them all, so young,
hair shiny, with their lives before them—
they were looking on me as a loser

and had no pity,
so determined were they
to make it big, to be winners.

Even the clerk in the social security office
looked at me with wonder and asked,
Have you always earned so little?

I had never thought of it that way—
to her too I was a loser,
with bad luck written all over my tax records.

What happened to the beautiful losers of my youth
who let the world destroy them
but stayed true to their dream,

scoffed at materialism, conventions,
a small, beleaguered band
who kept their integrity against the world
and devoted their lives
to Art, Sex, and Revolution?

Youth once believed in them, the madmen
who burned themselves out with drugs and drink,

disappeared into the desert,
or battered society with their shaggy heads.

There was one period even
when everybody was rushing off
in search of the Underground Man.

But now that winners are in fashion,
disappearing are the last of the bohemians,
left over from the old days of the Village,

and I am of another era, like the grizzled poet
who slept in Village doorways
and showed up at the Poetry Society
with his life work in a shopping bag

and read his poem "Crows":
Caw, caw, he cried,
as he jumped off a table,
flapping his arms.

Waiting for the Communists

after Cavafy's "Waiting for the Barbarians"

What's all the commotion about?
I haven't seen the city in such an upheaval
since the last power failure.

Haven't you heard? The communists are coming today.

Is that why so many people are packed into the stadium,
watching the giant television screens?

Yes, everyone wants to see what the communists look like.
Listen to them roaring for blood.

Why is Congress passing laws one after another
and the president, for once, not vetoing them
but signing them furiously?

Oh, they're making one more attempt to ban the communists.
But it won't do any good—when the communists get here
they'll make their own laws.

Why are government emissaries rushing to the harbor, the airport,
carrying pink-frosted cakes and party favors and hats?

Because that's the kind of junk they say communists like—
they're just barbarians, you know.

Why are the rich driving right behind them,
their wives in furs, arms and throats glittering with diamonds,
their cars loaded with opulent gifts—gold bars,
deeds to real estate, country club memberships?

Because the communists are coming today,
and they want to buy them off. They hope their elegant wives
will soften a little the hard hearts of the communists.

Why are the Supreme Court justices putting on their robes
and taking their places gravely on the bench?

Because after the government flees to its fortified island,
the judges will have to sign the surrender.

So why don't our big shots stand up now and make their speeches,
warn against the communists like they're always doing,
tell us how we must sacrifice, remain vigilant,
to protect our homes, our way of life?

Because the communists are finally coming
and nobody wants to listen to that stuff anymore.

But wait, why this outbreak of muttering in the crowds?
(How puzzled everyone looks, confused—even angry.)
See how the streets and squares are rapidly emptying,
and everybody going home so deep in thought.

Because it's evening and the communists haven't come.
And some people just back from abroad say
there aren't any communists anymore, maybe never were.

Oh my God, no communists?
Now what's going to happen?
You've got to admit they were the perfect solution.

Blinks

When you wind up a Helen Keller doll
what does it do?
It walks into the wall.

All blind jokes are anti-blind,
but it's true you've got to watch them like a hawk.
I look away for barely a second,
and there he is going off in a crazy direction.
He could get killed like that,
but there's an angel looking after them.

He used to hold onto my shoulder on the street
but doesn't like the image that gives him
(being blind doesn't make him less of a WASP),
so I am forced to steer him by his shoulder.
He likes that. I get taken for the blink.

A man holding another man's shoulder
doesn't raise an eyebrow in Italy,
or in the Moslem world where men walk hand in hand
and, if a man meets a friend and his wife,
shakes hands with the woman and kisses the man.
Even in England it's okay, the way we walk,
because everyone is too polite to notice.
Or in Holland, where no man would touch another in public,
no one would dream of making a remark.
Only in the States are we in danger,
where everything between men
is interpreted as sexual.
A good-hearted truck driver, stopping for a red light,
leaned out of his cab and shouted,
"Hey, watch out! AIDS!"
As if a hand on a shoulder could transmit the virus,

or perhaps he was nervous
one thing would lead to another.

But it's not always good-hearted, the attention.
To protect us from fag bashers I suggested
he carry his fold-up cane open so no one could miss it,
but this too would give him the wrong image.
Now, passing groups of kids, I half close my eyes
as if I were the blink, like a woman I know,
coming home on dark streets,
acts crazy to deter muggers and rapists.
If we start having real trouble,
I'll have to wear dark glasses and carry the cane.

Here's one that's not only anti-blind, but anti-guide dog:
>A woman saw a guide dog leading a blind man
>right into the moving traffic to cross the street.
>Getting to the other side, she was astonished to see
>the man feeding the dog a biscuit. "Excuse me, sir," she said,
>"why are you rewarding that dog? Don't you know he nearly
>got you killed?" "Sure," replied the blind man,
>"but I have to find out where his mouth is,
>so I can kick his ass."

As if foreshadowing his fate,
in childhood he invented a game with his sister:
Push the Blind Man into the Traffic.
Now he both hates the cane as the symbol
of his difference and rages against the sighted,
saying he'd like to strike out with it right and left,
just as I'd like to poke it into the wheels of bicycles
that whiz by and miss us by a hair.
He mutters again and again the words
of his mobility instructor at the blind school,
who taught him to negotiate the streets with a cane:
the world isn't set up for the blind.

Curious how the folded-up cane in his hand
is stared at by black people,
who take it for magic juju sticks or a weapon,
something for power.
Customs officials examine it as if its hollow shaft
was full of drugs, and one of them once asked
if it was karate sticks. Latinos
sometimes take it for a traffic warden's baton
and ask directions, which he, as an old New Yorker,
is perfectly able to give,
just as he can figure out where we are in London,
from the time when he could still see.

He'd like being blind to be classier
and imagines a Broadway musical, *Blinks on Parade*,
with a row of chorus boys in high-style mirrored sunglasses,
tapping their white canes back and forth to a jazzy beat,
though frequently it turns into a sci-fi/horror film,
called *Revenge of the Blinks*.

According to how they feel about the blind,
people, he claims, are either HB or AB.
Horror of the Blind is understandable.
Who wants to have to think about such a calamity!
They so often have off-putting blindisms
like rocking in place or grinning insanely.
And most people, hurrying on their way, resent
having to help the blind man at the curb,
who is helplessly banging his cane to be crossed.

It's always a relief to joke about it:
>   *What did Helen Keller's parents do to punish her,*
>   *rearrange the furniture?*
>   *No, they made her read the waffle iron.*

The other half of the race suffers
from AB, Adoration of the Blind.

African-Americans are the most afflicted
with this special sympathy, he says, even dope peddlers
will stop dealing and see that he gets safely by
a broken sidewalk, an obstacle, and even those
who resent whites will help him perhaps because
they are people with soul, and besides, they know
blinks have to be color-blind.

In Italy, people always try to sit him down,
though there's nothing wrong with his legs.
In fact, sitting down and eating
is what makes fatties of too many, though feeding them
is at least something you can do.
More serious, the world ignores their problems getting laid,
and for a long time, the books pushed on them
were spiritual works, perhaps to get their minds
off their horniness. Take it from me,
dirty books is what they want, if not sex clubs
and hustler services, to make it easier:
another blink I know hands out his card in the subway,
counting on his handicap for getting away with it,
though he's slightly defective besides.

In my role of guide I have to help daily
with a million little things—finding a slipper,
unjamming the tape player, spreading peanut butter,
combing his hair. At all times you have to be prepared
for a crash, and yelling, Don't Move!,
race to sweep up the shattered glass.
How powerful, clever, useful, and virtuous
that makes me feel, with my eyes
that solve so many problems, and then furious
when he isn't grateful, or when he doesn't
catch on to something I'm explaining, the dumb blink—
perfectly simple, with eyes, or I'm offended
when he lets me have it for telling him how to do things.
He particularly resents

my taking his finger and trying to guide it
to the right button on the tape player, for instance.
He also gives it to me for moving things
so he can't find them, and it's even my fault,
when he walks into me, for being in the way.
But then, I nearly give him a heart attack
if I speak when he thinks I'm out of the room.

They have a perfect right to hate us,
but somebody has to tell him
when it's a curb or wheelchair ramp,
or when there's a hole or dogshit on the sidewalk,
or a head-level metal sign or low-hanging branch,
or a little dog or child he might step on.
"Veer left," I'm always saying, and it annoys him
to take orders, because it's his nature
to be the one in charge, or he complains
when I warn him too late, his foot
already in the air over the precipice.
Luckily he has a strong back—
mine would have been in a brace long ago.

Even if I sound disenchanted, half-agreeing
with those who say, "Shit,
better put them out of their fucking misery,"
or sometimes muttering, "I'd kill myself if I was blind,"
I've got an incurable case of AB,
for as sighted guide, I found,
after lonely years of near suicidal misery,
my role in life, helper,
or as I sometimes feel about it, slave.
It's a lot of work, full time without a break,
if you're thinking of going for it, baby,
and unlike seeing-eye dogs, who are sent
to a farm in the country when they get old and tired,
I'll probably drop dead in harness.

Dietrich

She never had to make up
for not being popular at school—
she started out well beyond all that.

She was never a bobby-soxer, for example,
nor one of those girls fighting
against going all the way—
you don't go from that to where she is.

When she sings "My ideal is a big blond man"
or "Every night another bliss"
you know just what she means by this.

Ancient in Paris,
perfect setting for monuments
where the boulevards culminate
in a granite bust,

where the populace adores
the will that invents
an inviolable mask—
still she writes "This rotten world,"

as if tied to a mast and forced
to witness, as she always has,
her eyes windows
with the shades permanently up.

Hear, O Israel

At age sixty-four, waking in the night
not with a hard-on, alas, but indigestion,
I, son of Jews from the shtetls of Poland and Russia,
of a father with the eagle profile of a sheik
and a mother with a goyish nose,
give my testimony for the Moslem world,
maligned as fanatic and backward, even evil.

What a privilege to have been to Morocco,
where people are robed like in the Bible,
and over the high Atlas to the Sahara,
the beginning of the silk route to Asia . . .
and Tunisia with desert roads that end
in salt flats or an oasis, that's the chance you have to take
when you set out on your journey,

and to have breathed in the dust of Cairo,
the germ repository of the Nile . . .
and holy Jerusalem, built over a spiritual fault
that can never allow peace, but heightens the spirit . . .
and beyond, the long overland route to Afghanistan on a bus,
with intimations of the Gobi Desert and China in the nostrils.

My God, how much I've learned in that world,
not least, that I was a man.
Those Wise Ones, they look in your eyes and see what you're worth,
and I don't mean in camels or Cadillacs—though baksheesh,
a gift, is never amiss.
Still, they are the ones who always give gifts,
making one's soul flower in gratitude.

That world that feeds the soul taught me
that I was a man and had a soul, and if mine

is a tormented one, at least it experienced itself fully
on the journey through the desert, squatting
in the slender shadow of a palm tree, of a broken-down bus,
or among oleanders with robed men,
drinking mint tea bees hover over.

It is a world where, unlike ours, men like each other,
where, looking deep into your eyes,
men are not afraid to take your hand
and say, Come stranger, break thy journey and linger awhile
so that we may open our lives, our hearts to each other,
before we move on refreshed. . . .

How many times have I lugged my valise
through the turmoil of peddlers at the bus depot,
down a dusty road, past shops and hovels closed up
in the midday heat, past long walls
that shut you out absolutely, revealing only
white domes against a blue sky
and a minaret with loudspeakers
for the recorded muezzin call at prayer times,
or sometimes even a white-clad figure on the high balcony,
chanting to the four corners of the town
for all to come and pray—
a long, weary trek.

Any voyage there begins at dawn and lasts all day,
but after dust and thirst, you might arrive
at green palm groves crisscrossed with rivulets,
and at the heart a blue pool
where holy beggars are washing themselves
and someone is always doing his laundry.
There is somehow a hotel nearby
or at least a tea shop to come out of the sun, a melon
to share, and coarse desert bread one could live on.
It is of its essence

that after you go beyond despair,
lugging that damn suitcase in the sun,
plagued by beggars and flies,
surrounded only by desolation, poverty, and waste,
and are ready to give up,
this world can transform itself
from a garbage dump into a garden,
enveloping you in attar of roses.

On my floors are rugs I have brought back,
a bit of . . . The Mysterious East.
Here, where so much is phony, the wool retains
something of the caravan, the nomad flocks,
that makes cats go crazy on it.
Woven into the patterns with bits of straw and dung
are fragments of a forgotten language, glimmers
of meaning . . . about ancestry, about honor, memories
of our history even, that special strand
reminding me what Jew means:
one who remembers, one who has it woven
into his being to remember.

Tonight, with the Shema—Hear, O Israel—on his lips,
let this old Jew give his tribute to the Moslem world,
that has preserved our connections to ourselves,
to the old times, that can remind us
what we have lost, that can still
teach us what we were, who we are.

Hear me, Israel, before the insanity of the world,
the lack of love for our brothers,
leads to the destruction of us all.

I seal this testimony with a kiss
to my soul's beloved, my sacred brother, as we embrace
with beating hearts in the long night.

Trop Tard Pour Paris

Returning to France after years,
I can only feel regret
for a life I never lived.
Too late now, I say, *trop tard,*
trop tard pour Paris.

But maybe a part of me didn't leave
in the long ago of my youth
when, broke, I signed on the freighter home
but stayed behind as a kind of ghost
to live a parallel life to mine.

Here, in the so-familiar Parisian air
is still the suspicion of a ghostly me,
skinny as ever, unchangeably stubborn and young,
who never got on that boat, and unlike me,
didn't need money or a job to stay,

and while I lived out my New York life,
—analysts, transient loves, the years—
my Other floated through the terrible mists
of the city he could never bear to leave,
the only place he could ever feel at home.

And yet, by giving up Paris I gained
the rest of the world, it's true, though I know
it's here I should have lived my life.
Now it's too late, too late for me,
trop tard pour Paris.

The Last Bohemians

for Rosetta Reitz

We meet in a cheap diner and I think, God,
the continuity, I mean, imagine
our still being here together
from the old days of the Village
when you had the bookshop on Greenwich Avenue
and Jimmy Baldwin and Jimmy Merrill used to drop in.

Toying with your gooey chicken, you remind me
how disappointed I was with you for moving
to Eighth Street and adding gifts and art cards,
but little magazines, you explain, couldn't pay the rent.
Don't apologize, I want to say, it was forty years ago!

Neither of us, without clinging to our old apartments,
could pay Village rents nowadays,
where nobody comes "to be an artist" anymore.
Living marginally still, we are shabby as ever,
though shabby was attractive on us once—those years
when the latest Williams or Stevens or Moore was sold
in maybe five bookstores, and the Horton
biography of Hart Crane an impossible find.
Continuity! We're still talking of our problems
with writing, finding a publisher,
as though that was the most important thing in the world.
Sweetheart, we are as out of it as old lefties.

Someone came into my apartment recently and exclaimed,
"Why, it's bohemian!" as if she had discovered
the last of a near-extinct breed.
Lady, I wanted to protest,
I don't have clamshell ashtrays,
or Chianti bottles encrusted with candle wax,

or Wilhelm Reich, Henry Miller, and D. H. Lawrence,
much less Kahlil Gibran and Havelock Ellis,
on my bricks-and-boards bookshelves!
But it's not just the Salvation Army junk she saw
or the mattress and pillows on the floor.
My living style represented for her
the aesthetic of an earlier generation,
the economics, even, of a time,
our time, Rosetta, before she was born.

The youth still come weekends, though not to
"see a drag show,"
or "bull daggers fighting in the gutters,"
or to "pick up a queer or artist's model."
But there is something expectant in them
for something supposed to be here, once called,
(shiver) bohemian. Now it's I who shiver
as I pass them, fearing their rage against
an old guy with the sad face of a loser.
Daytime, it's safer, with couples in from the suburbs
browsing the antique shops.
I find it all so boring, but am stuck here,
a ghost in a haunted house.

At a movie about a war criminal whose American
lawyer daughter blindly defends him, blasted by the critics
because it is serious and has a message,
the audience is full of old Villagers, drawn to see it
because it's serious and has a message,
the women, no longer in dirndls and sandals,
but with something telltale about the handcrafted jewelry,
the men not in berets, but the kind that would wear them,
couples for whom being young meant being radical,
meant free love. Anyway,
something about them says Villager,

maybe the remnants of intellect, idealism,
which has begun to look odd on American faces.

Nowadays, there's nothing radical left, certainly not
in the Village, no Left Bank to flee to, no justification
for artistic poverty, nothing for the young to believe in,
except their careers and the fun of flaunting
their youth and freaky hairstyles in trendy enclaves.

Leftovers from the old Village, we spot each other
drifting through the ghostly
high-rental picturesque streets, ears echoing
with typewriters clacking and scales and arpeggios
heard no more, and meet fugitive in coffee shops,
partly out of friendship, but also, as we get shabbier and rarer,
from a sense of continuity like, hey, we're historic!
and an appreciation, even if we never quite got there,
of what our generation set out to do.

World Traveler

On the shore of the Caspian Sea
I sobbed to be so far away,
and across the plains of Turkestan,
passing camel caravans, I wept,
and in the high Pamirs, and among the ruins
of Balkh, Mother of Cities.

Desolation filled me as I saw
everywhere the men
out walking, holding hands
or with arms around each other,
friends kissing on street corners.

Why wasn't I happy?
I had come to where men
were as I was, or rather where what I was
was one of the possibilities of a man.

This was the world of my ancestors
—I knew it in my bones—
ancestors whose language was lost,
and my bones were announcing
that I had suffered for nothing,
been punished for nothing.
Not only my parents had been crazy,
but where I grew up was crazy—
no one could tell me different now,
I thought, as I picked up a blue tile
from the ruins and tucked it in my pocket,
rich with newfound treasures.

But no matter that I knew—
and the further I went the more I knew—
I sobbed and sobbed, for what had been done
could not, in this lifetime at least,
be undone.

Rule of the Desert

1.

All night on the bus, crowded three to a seat—
the government bus a bargain—
the metal edge of the window rubbed my elbow raw.
Over and over, through the dry heat of the desert night,
I said the 23rd Psalm . . . *green pastures . . . still waters.*

Hours of this, until a midnight rest stop
for tea under trees strung with dim lights
by a dark hotel, alone on the vast, barren plain.
A Russian resort, the waiter said,
but they came only in winter.
And *over there?* I asked, pointing to a wall.
The swimming pool, he said.
Full? I asked.
Of course, he said.

A pool? But I had no bathing suit, no towel,
and we'd be leaving in a few minutes,
the night-long drive ahead. I sat,
thirst unquenched by the tea, the last orange
from Herat. Debated. Yes . . . No . . . Impossible.
Then walked over to the wall
where a line of turbaned men from the bus
were sitting, waiting for departure, and sure enough,
there was a swimming pool, deserted, dark.
At once, I was over the wall, sweaty clothes off,
and slipped into the water—pure water from springs
far beneath the desert, silvery in moonlight.
Not a turbaned head turned round.

On the bus again, instantly dry in the desert air,
I pondered the miracle of it—after hours of prayer,
a Russian swimming pool in the desert?
Still, this was the East, where mysterious
things can happen—one minute beggar, king the next.
And perhaps here, if you pray correctly—if, if,
allowing for many ifs and not expecting anything,
certain prayers might be answered.

2.

After that, no one would talk to me
except a French girl, going to stay with nuns,
who asked to sit next to me for protection.

By the others, I was made to feel
I had disgraced myself with violations
of dignity, modesty, manliness.
There are rules in the civilized world,
and even if I was a tourist
(the driver muttered the word), wasn't I a man?

Clearly, the French girl was also disgraced,
sitting as she was with me in the men's section,
the worse offender, even,
and by association, a whore.

But by the time the bus broke down at dawn
and before we were picked up by another,
I was forgiven. The men nudged me, grinning,
saying, "How many times?"
indicating the frightened girl,
now properly up front with the veiled women,
as I was in back with the heavy-breathing men.

Sex Among the Savages

in memoriam Tobias Schneebaum

Letters from an adventurous friend describe
his visits to a naked Stone Age tribe
(all smeared with pig fat and for my tastes skinny)
surviving in the forests of New Guinea.

My friend explores what is usually missed
by the explorer or the scientist.
Enough, then, about carved shields and deadly spears,
spiral inserts for the nose and ears,
which make the tribesmen unglamorously fierce,
or foot-long penis sheathes they wear erect
that anthropologists eagerly collect—
things with which I've always been slightly bored
and the secrets I want to hear about ignored.

Now my friend confirms what one suspects:
There's more to primitive life than artifacts,
or head-hunting, or eating human brains—
though he assures me a lot of that remains.

The missionaries claim they've wiped it out,
but he's learned from his Stone Age friends, first-hand, about
one of the ancient traditions that endure:
this holds that a boy can't properly mature
unless he drinks an unspecified amount,
but the more the better, of jungle gism
spurting fresh and joyful from the fount—
good, they believe, for a boy's metabolism.
What's more, the future of the tribes depended
on keeping their boys kneeling or upended.
So the men of this people wisely do their best,

my friend writes, in the tribal interest
by shooting a load as often as they can,
and this way the boy learns to be a man.

Pig fat and all, the primitive world of sex,
for those, like my friend, with the nerve to risk their necks.

Callas

The voice that came out of her
chose her as its earthly vehicle,
for reasons only the gods can know.

She spoke of it as separate from her, a wild creature
she had to struggle to master.

It floats like an unwieldy bird with a small head
whose wings can't quite control the over-large body
soaring dangerously low above jagged peaks,
wobbling in the updrafts.

Like an Egyptian sculpture of a priestess,
she held up her large, arresting hands,
invoking the authority of the ancients—
hawks, serpents, bulls, and suns surrounded her as she sang,
cut into stone.

She had that specialized genius for song
birds have, an intelligence of too high a vibration
for the practical matters of life.
But she was unfaithful to her gift—
even if for the understandable reasons
of being fashionable and getting a man—
otherwise she would never have dieted down,
but stayed fat for those spectacular tones,
living only for art.

It was an operatic fate
that the man she suffered over
was one of the great rats
who dismissed the most magnificent voice in the world

as just a whistle in her throat.
But after her sexless marriage, this was probably
the first man with a hard-on she got together with,
and duck-like, fixated on,
as is so common with us ordinary slobs.
With some men, whatever they are besides, the cock
is the best part of them, even if they are monsters
and, like him, supremely ruthless.
And perhaps his selfishness is what ravished her,
for it was sexuality in the raw, the one thing
singing wasn't.

Like Norma, the Druid nun, who broke her vows
for the love of a mere mortal,
she, too, was cast aside,
not for any high priestess, but a more earthly rival,
famous widow, jet-set icon,
who didn't need his powerful cock, just his power,
and a big allowance.

She threw away her magic voice for a man who threw her away—
thunderclap in the heavens, an accusing dagger of lightning—
and her crystal brain—
whose single-minded command like a bird's
was to soar, to sing—
shattered, and she fell.

The Guide

How I loved the high country, the snow, and the cold,
and with such pure air it was exhilarating,
the two of us setting off across the valley
dotted with clumps of spruce,
and even with his handicap, it was easy
to guide him through the deep, powdery snow
that the wind blew up in our faces.

Then the land rose, and with his handicap
the going got harder, but he held onto my shoulder,
and we slogged on to the top
where we stopped, breathless: below, at my feet,
was a terrible, almost perpendicular, drop
into a landscape shattered by some ancient cataclysm,
a jumble of rocks with dangerous crevices
hidden by snow, and twisted trees
clinging everywhichway.

I stood there, aghast, and calculated:
we could camp here overnight,
but even if we managed, holding on,
to slide and tumble down the slope
without breaking anything,
and by some miracle end up together,
how, with his handicap, could I guide him
through the rocky terrain ahead—though I knew
there was no way to go, but on?

Garbo

Her eyes never blink—
higher beings do not blink,

nor people in remote lands
who stare at you from the fields—
but that's innocence, like animals.

If blinking is a kind of flinching,
she never flinches.
She doesn't adopt any facial expression—
it's her feelings she shows
or none at all. Nor does she put on
mannerisms like we do, meaning
we're desperate for attention.
If she says she wants to be alone
she's the only one we believe it of.

It's no devices then that make her beautiful
but the lack of them. Still, the awkwardness
of her grace shows that being graceful
is not an easy victory—
there's that permanent mournfulness in the mouth
and the testimony of those eyes—
no blinking back,
it's all there.

Can't we make the same commitment,
risk shedding evasions, devices, defenses
—in short, our faces—
and look unblinking at each other, vulnerable
to what in our hearts we long for,
whatever the cost, wherever it leads?

Or does she affirm that for mere mortals
the price is too great,
though for herself
she could not, would not, choose another fate.

from *A Frieze for a Temple of Love, Poems 1993–1997*

(1998)

Colombian Gold

On a Colombian folktale
told to me by Jaime Manrique

1

On the day God
created the earth,
all the angels
flew round and round,
singing chorales
of praise.

But over one place
they stopped,
beating the air
with their angel wings,
as their inspired voices
rose to heaven.
Here alone, they trilled,
is paradise on earth
and it's called
Colombia!

Yes, God said,
beaming at them
wickedly,
but wait till tomorrow
and see
who I'm going
to populate it with.

2

On the day
God created the earth,
all the angels
flew round and round, singing
chorales of praise.

Day after day they celebrated
as God produced from his fingertips
plants and creatures,
and, according to an ancient tradition,
in a final burst of genius,
a diadem of cities.

A chorus of hallelujahs
rose from the angels
over the glitter
of Paris, London, Rome,
until fluttering in convoy
over Columbia, District of,
they looked down in awe
at God's masterpiece,
a perfect gem of a city
with domed capitol and avenues
radiating like the rays
around the crown of Athena,
Goddess of Wisdom.

Hail to the city of Washington,
the angels sang,
from whose marble temples
and pillared halls
the people will be justly governed
and an eternity of goodness
reign over the earth.

Don't be too sure, said God
with his slyest grin.
Wait till tomorrow
and see who I populate it with.

And then I'm going to
do nothing for the rest of time
but sit back and laugh,
watching what happens.

My Sister, the Queen

Walking the broad allée past Kensington Palace,
more like a country house, really, than a palace,
where a young Queen Victoria
presides gracefully in stone over royal lawns
sweeping down to the distant mockery
of Henry Moore's giant marble thighbones,

I half expect to see at an upper window
a familiar figure looking out,
the once-pretty face tear- and mascara-stained,
whiskey glass in hand, chain-smoking the cigarettes
forbidden her since the operation.

For a modern Queen, there are more ways than one
to keep a prettier, wilder sister under control
besides locking her in the Tower,
and this one did not hesitate to use her power
to prevent her from marrying
a divorced man, and a commoner to boot,
forcing on her, instead, a loveless marriage
that ended, like a slap in the royal face,
in divorce.

This may be the time, though, when threats
no longer silence her, and I imagine I see
the wretched Princess at the window,
her glass empty and with nothing more to lose,
throwing open the sash and screaming to the world
how her sister has ruined her life.
But just as she is about to hurl herself out,
experienced hands grab her from behind
to clamp over the twisted, hysterical mouth,

and drag her, struggling like a wounded moth,
back inside, where the doctor
waits with the hypodermic,

and as the window slams shut again,
and the heavy drapes, embroidered by the hands
of her sister, the Queen, are drawn,
I blink away the vision
and continue my walk
through the unearthly gardens.

Magic Words

on an Inuit theme

In the very earliest times,
when both people and animals
lived on earth,
a PERSON could become
an ANIMAL
if he wanted to,
and an ANIMAL
could become a HUMAN BEING.

Sometimes we were
PEOPLE
and sometimes
ANIMALS
and there was no difference—
all spoke the same,
the UNIVERSAL TONGUE.

That was a time
when WORDS were like
MAGIC.
The mind had
MYSTERIOUS POWERS,
and a word uttered by chance
might have
CONSEQUENCES.

It would suddenly
COME ALIVE,
and what people wanted to happen
COULD HAPPEN—
all you had to do was
SAY IT.

Nobody could explain it.
That's just the way
it was.

It's one of those old things
that has been
forgotten,
LOST
the way a pebble
drops
from the hand of a child.

How can we FIND it again
to make things happen
that we want to happen,

HEAL the sick,
FEED the hungry,
HOUSE the homeless,
and HELP
the suffering?

How to find
the syllables
buried deep within us,
the MAGIC WORDS,

TO LIVE

IN PEACE

WITH THE ANIMALS

AGAIN?

Colossus

It's awesome to have straddled a century,
lived through the peak years of an empire,
that brief period
of absolute supremacy, unlimited wealth,
then The Decline, and inescapably,
The Fall,
which now looks sooner rather than later.
My country, perhaps we'll crash down together,
and it will be up to archaeologists
of some unimaginable future
to figure out how the chunks fit
and which belong to me or it.

It's the classical pattern:
victory in war brought such power
we could have created a golden age on earth,
had wise men ruled,
but, predictably,
our riches were never used wisely.
As if hungry, we just became
a devouring monster.
In the wrong hands, everything,
the gifts of the gods,
was wasted.

Corrupt and paranoid,
our rulers created a world
of two blocs locked in struggle,
Good versus Evil.
In the name of freedom, we assassinated,
here and abroad, the very people
who might have done the world some good,

and destroyed everything we couldn't control—
other opinions, simple debate, difference—
and were also clever enough
to debase the popular mind,
as well as intellectual thought,
by branding generosity of spirit subversive.

That was the dogma we lived by,
so when the other side collapsed,
ours, wealth squandered, corrupt,
was left with a dubious victory.

Awesome to have lived through this drama,
the rise and fall of an empire,
and now, with ignorance more entrenched than ever
and threatening to unleash
final suicidal destruction on the planet,
I, still shakily astride my century, wait
to crumble into ruins with it.

St. Petersburg, 1918

in memory of the USSR

You were sitting on a grassy hummock
by the river as the children
played around you. The water
was flowing lazily.
It was spring,
a perfect day.
I hardly knew who you were,
my mother or what,
it didn't matter.

Across, on the other bank,
young athletes leapt from heights,
lithe in the air,
practicing for the games.
You said you wanted to burn all our money.
I knew it was not so much from idealism
as despair, and I held you
and asked you not to.

It was before everything that happened.
The purges were still to come.
How we believed in the revolution!
That was our youth.
Foolish tears run down my face.
My house of love
would never be so full.

The Bukowski Option

in memoriam Charles Bukowski

An old guy has two choices:
     the Bukowski Option,
which allows you to express all your nastier impulses
     and tell the world to go fuck itself—
this is the Way of Purity, the Bohemian Ideal,
     with its vow never to Sell Out.
On the other hand, whether you sell out or don't,
     you can try, in your old age,
for the discipline of Dignity,
     which is made more difficult
     when you have to take a leak
and every restaurant has a sign in the window,
     "Toilet for customers only."

I lived most of my life as a freak,
     which expressed my contempt
     for the capitalist system.
Eventually, though, I too opted for Dignity
     as a protection and disguise
for my battered dreams—
     ideals I still believe in.

But, I ask myself,
     don't you want to be a rebel anymore,
     an example to youth?
Yes, but I'm too dismayed
     by that sagging face in the mirror
and too conceited
     to look like I have dirty underwear
or droopy pants like a full diaper.
     Even Buk didn't grow a beard,
which would at least have saved his five

most wasted minutes of the day, shaving,
and even have covered the scars
        of acne, drink, and time.
But his beauty was
        that he insisted on thrusting
his entire ugly face in our faces,
        which was tremendously entertaining, of course,
and he knew it,
        even as he snarled at the world.

Can you take the Bukowski Option, I wonder,
        and not turn into a wreck?
What would it be like, I wonder,
        to live like a slob,
and smoke my head off, drink,
        and eat junk food?
I'm too much of a hypochondriac.
        But at some point, maybe,
when there's nothing left to lose?
        As my mother always said,
When you need a drink, you need a drink.
        That time, at least, has come—
frequently.

The Dignified Option would seem to mean
        staying out of sight,
maybe retiring to the country,
        except it's too boring,
especially with the old back
        ruling out gardening.
A composer I knew, like the man without a face,
        would only go out at night
to take long bus rides
        through deserted neighborhoods.
What the hell was he supposed to do?
        Dignity is a good way

of disappearing, then even in public
　　no one will notice you.
They're all just thankful the old wreck
　　isn't being a troublemaker.

But even as a Dignified Gent, it's a constant
　　struggle not to be nasty,
because you don't have to be Bukowski
　　to have a ball of hatred and disgust
in your gut for the world.
　　Though unlike him I'll admit
I'm a sucker for lovey-dovey people.
　　Still, I wonder about the pixyish codgers
with their wispy hair and illumined eyes,
　　playing giggling Chinese sages
as if old age was a barrel of laughs.
　　They've either found something I haven't,
or are frauds.
　　I'd guess the latter.

I cringe when I think of that librarian, once,
　　cooing at my shrunken, ancient father
and him twinkling back, playing her game. Pitiful!
　　Nasty would be better,
like dropping a loud fart, for example,
　　in the hush of the library.
The woman at the supermarket checkout counter
　　who automatically makes two bags for me—
while I think I'm getting points for being Dignified,
　　she knows all about old men's prostates,
however good an act I put on.
　　Leaving a puddle on the floor
would be a satisfying slap in her face
　　for reading me like a book,
and with the long walk home ahead, a relief,
　　even with wet pants leg flapping.

My lament is this,
  that any dog anytime
is free to squat
  or lift its leg to pee,

and on the street Bukowski
  or any normal freak
would simply turn to a wall and take
  a necessary leak,

which sometimes makes it seem
  that my worst mistake
was choosing
  Dignity.

You win,
  Bukowski.

from "A Man and His Penis"

Old Acquaintance

> *Deirdre! Come out!*
> *Come out from behind that screen.*
> *I've been hiding behind screens*
> *since before you were born.*
>
> —Bette Davis, in *Old Acquaintance*

Old friend, we've come through
in pretty good shape, so far,
better, in fact,
than during those angst-filled years
when you wrecked my life
and I wrecked yours. Remember?
But, back then, we didn't appreciate each other,
did we—like an ill-matched couple,
a bad job by an incompetent marriage broker,
or who just got married out of general horniness
rather than any real compatibility.

I never liked your looks or size,
and you had ideas of your own
I couldn't figure out,
though I responded to your goading
and roamed the nights away.
My God, what you led me into,
and I got you into some pretty tight fixes myself.

Life is less strenuous now.
In our golden years, you make few demands.
We've both come to like a bit of a wank,
with none of the old recriminations after.

And I've even learned to admire,
as I pose in the mirror,
your silky length,
respect your sulky independence.
I wonder that I ever thought you
insufficient, myself under-endowed—
or else you've grown.

Best of all, I'm impressed
by how good we look together—
the proportions seem just right.
So, Good Cock,
dick, prick, dong,
lul, bite, schwantz,
wang, willie, weenie,
and all your other names,
if you've a mind to, now,
and I'd say you've earned it,
stand up, old friend, with me
and take a bow.

from "My Life as a Dog"

Power Source

Like harnessing
the tides
or the wind,
how about attaching
dogs' tails
to power generators?

I want the job
of patting the dog
to keep its tail
wagging and wagging!

We'll illuminate
whole cities,
countries—
together, we'll
light up the world!

Sorry, I Never Slept with Allen Ginsberg

What poet does not rejoice
at the death of a poet—
like the young princess,
who studied the line of succession.
"I am closer to the throne
than I had thought," she said.
Still a child, it was in her blood
to consider doing
a Richard the Third herself
to clear her path.
Even I, taking up as little space as possible,
am blocking others,
the hungry, the unpublished,
behind me, saying,
"Get the hell out of my way."

Allen Ginsberg took up a lot of space.
Relieved now at his absence,
we are all the more eager
to praise him into stone,
embalm him in sainthood.
The only trouble is
that in death as in life
he is protean—
he spreads everywhere now.
Our country has an immense
debt of gratitude to him,
for it was his lone voice,
half crazy but unmistakable,
that announced the end
of the reign of terror in the fifties,
an Age of Injustice,

when they actually got almost everybody
to believe that this country
was about to be taken over
by a handful of lefties,

when free thought
was made a crime,
with black lists, imprisonment, and executions—

the mad doctor, Wilhelm Reich, dying in jail,
his books and orgone boxes burned,
because he preached good sex as a cure,

the Rosenbergs
fried in the electric chair
for being communists,

homosexuals declared dangerous
to national security,
hunted down and fired from their jobs,
even lobotomized,

university teachers
forced to sign loyalty oaths,

writers, actors, and directors sent to jail,
denied passports,
forbidden to work,

and the great Paul Robeson
ruined—

when the entire creative world of the left
turned against itself,
proving their patriotism
in denouncing each other.

How gloomy was the Village in those years,
the San Remo bar nearly deserted,
with everyone going to their analysts—
as if we could cure the world on the couch.

Then came "Howl,"
a cry of defiance,
declaring the right to be whatever we are,
a mere poem that destroyed the destroyers,
the haters,
the killers in our government,
and gave courage to the oppressed.
Everything started coming alive again.
The courts allowed banned books
to be published,
Mayor Lindsay stopped the police
from raiding gay bars,
and liberation was in the air.
Though nothing could heal the damage done
from the fear of intelligence
implanted by the witch-hunters
in the national psyche—

a permanent trauma
that only one Allen Ginsberg
couldn't heal.
Though he tried.

This uncircumcised Jew,
with his Old Testament voice,
in the best Jewish tradition,
was completely down to earth,
a mensch.
When he gave a reading in Miami Beach
at my sister's neighborhood temple,
she called out over the crush of

adoring matrons around him,
"Allen, my brother is Edward Field,"
and he answered with the gentlest of mockery,
"Hello, Edward Field's Miami Beach sister."
He even reduced top poetry critic Helen Vendler,
who had to detest his messy poems,
to coy, shivering approval—
though that was more the Politics of Power
rather than any yielding to the genuine.

Throughout the cold war
he remained faithful
to his communist mother,
though his own communism was not
the rigid, puritanical variety
but a kind that has room for all of us,
that wants us to be ourselves.
He belonged to a bohemian left
the witch-hunters
could never understand
when they put artists and thinkers in jail—
a left that included
sex and astrology,
Buddhist chanting and modern dance
and marijuana.
If it's real communism
it should let everybody live.

I hardly knew Allen Ginsberg,
but since we're from the same generation and queer,
I'm always asked by the young
if I ever went to bed with him.
Since he's no longer around to deny it,
I think I'll start saying I did,
though I'm pretty sure we weren't each other's type.
I don't think he'd mind.

He liked saying, "I've had him,"
about everybody famous,
or just anybody—he took sex as a right.
Gary Lenhart once reported
after getting in the sack with him
that Ginsberg made love
"in a friendly fashion."

The rich and famous,
like Jacqueline Kennedy Onassis,
don't have to die in agony.
It's pretty clear
that after the fatal diagnosis
his death, like hers,
was helped along.
All over the country there is agreement,
if it's hopeless,
why not help end the suffering
before it becomes unbearable?
But the government won't listen.
Still, nobody objects
that in AIDS, at the unbearable stage,
you will be given morphine drip,
if the family approves.

Even our most famous poet,
world famous,
you don't expect the Nobel Prize
if you shoot your mouth off like he did.
But surely Poet Laureate?
No, even there—too queer, too radical.
The government would rather play it safe
with tame, academic poets
who keep their mouths shut
about injustice—
all of them, to date,
straight.

On his death
his government didn't honor him
as any civilized country would have.
There were no mass funeral processions,
the president made no official eulogy
about the loss to the nation,
proclaimed no moment of silence.
There was no resting place
for his ashes
in a pantheon of the great.

He didn't need any of that.
When he died,
the earth shook.

Acknowledgments

Some of these poems have been published in *Barrow Street, The Best American Poetry 2005, Big Bridge, Chiron Review, Fire (UK), 5 AM, Gay & Lesbian Review, Hamilton Stone Review, Hanging Loose, Lasting: Poems on Aging, Margie, MiPOesias Magazine* (the David Trinidad Edition, 2007), *Poetry Calendar 2007, Solo, Tears in the Fence (UK), Tikkun, William and Mary Review, Witness.*